Santa Biblia

Santa Biblia

The Bible Through Hispanic Eyes

Justo L. González

Abingdon Press
Nashville

SANTA BIBLIA: The Bible Through Hispanic Eyes

Copyright © 1996 by Abingdon Press

This book is printed on recycled, acid-free paper.

Library of Congress Cataloging-in-Publication Data

González, Justo L.
    Santa Biblia: the Bible through Hispanic eyes/Justo L. González.
        p.   cm.
    Includes bibliographical references.
    ISBN 0-687-01452-2 (alk. paper)
        1.   Bible—Hermeneutics.   2. Liberation theology.   3. Hispanic American theology.
    4. Bible—Criticism, interpretation, etc.
    I. Title.
    BS476.G66   1996
    220.6'089'68—dc20   95-37833
                                                                                          CIP

01 02 03 04 05—10 9 8 7 6 5 4 3

MANUFACTURED IN THE UNITED STATES OF AMERICA

CONTENTS

I n some very concrete ways, this book is the result of the work of
the Mexican American Program at Perkins School of Theology
and of its Director, Dr. Roy D. Barton. In 1975, Dr. Barton
convened a group of pastors and professors, under what he called
the Hispanic Instructors Program. This group has met at least
annually since its inception and has enriched the Hispanic church
in many ways. Designed originally as a nurturing and support
program for people who could teach in various settings, the Hispanic
Instructors soon began to enhance the courses taught at Perkins with
their own Hispanic perspective, and their meetings also became a
forum for discussing the best curriculum, courses, and bibliography
for the Spanish language Course of Study offered at Perkins every
summer. Then, other projects emerged either as direct by-products
of the Instructors' meetings, or at least supported by them: the
journal *Apuntes,* for a long time the only journal of Hispanic
theology in the United States, and now in its fifteenth year of
publication; a series of symposia on a variety of themes, culminating
on a series of three symposia under the common title of "Redescubrimiento," planned around the theme of the Quincentennial of

1492; programs for the training of laity in theology and in the practice of ministry; and many more.

As the Redescubrimiento project drew to a close, the Instructors discussed a number of themes that had emerged and that should be pursued further. One of these themes was biblical interpretation, and included both an exploration of the manner in which Latinos interpret the Scripture, and the desire to make a contribution, out of our own experience, to the entire church's understanding of at least some biblical passages.

With that end in mind, a procedure was designed. This consisted, first of all, in inviting the Instructors as well as others to submit to the office of the Mexican American Program at least one written piece—a sermon, Bible lesson, portion of a commentary—in which they felt that their own Hispanic experience and commitment had resulted in an insight into the biblical text that was somehow different from the more common interpretations, and was also worthy of being shared with the church at large.[1] Having read these materials, the Instructors met both in small groups and in plenary sessions, analyzing what they had read, and trying to elucidate the elements, as well as the particular instances, of a Hispanic biblical hermeneutic that should be shared with a wider public.

I was asked to take notes of those meetings, and on that basis as well as on the basis of materials written by other Latinos, to write a book for publication by Abingdon Press. The first draft of the manuscript was then shared with the Instructors, who in their December meeting in 1994 made comments and suggestions for its improvement. On the basis of those comments and suggestions, the final draft was produced.

This means that this book is both a communal enterprise and a very personal one. It is communal in that it has resulted from the ideas of a community that has been gathering over the years to discuss issues such as those addressed in this book. Many of those ideas, first expressed by one of our members, have been so shaped by our discussion that it would be extremely difficult to assign them any longer to a particular person. In those cases where my notes clearly indicate who said something, I have tried to acknowledge that fact.

I have done the same when referring to written materials—in the case of published materials, I have given the appropriate bibliographical data, and in the case of unpublished materials, I have simply mentioned the author. But the fact remains that most of the ideas expressed in the pages that follow are communal, having been shaped by an interaction that gave rise to views and insights none of us could have developed by ourselves. The same is true for the Latino community at large. Much of what is said here are ideas that I have developed in conversation with friends and colleagues from that community. They are ideas that I would never have developed were it not for the insights and support derived from such conversations. Therefore, they are my ideas and insights in the sense that I claim them as valid, and not necessarily in the sense that I claim them as my own production.

But this book is also very personal. It is personal because, after all, a person is an individual existing in community. It is personal because, even though many of the ideas expressed herein were not originally mine, they have affected and shaped me in a very personal way. And it is personal because my agreement with the other Hispanic Instructors was that, although I would listen to their comments and suggestions, in the end I would be ultimately responsible for whatever was said, and not try to produce a book of such bland shapelessness that they could all agree with everything that was being said—like a committee report!

I thank Roy Barton and the rest of the Hispanic Instructors for the many insights I have received during these years, and most especially for the challenge and the opportunity to write this book. In particular, I wish to thank those colleagues who took the time to read the first draft of the manuscript, and to offer detailed suggestions and corrections: Edgar Avitia, María Luisa Santillán-Baert, Irving Cotto, Roberto Gómez, Pablo Jiménez, Loida Martell-Otero, and José David Rodríguez. Thanks to their efforts, this book has been significantly improved. I trust that through it the reader will gain some new insights, not only into what the Latino Christian community has to say, but also into what the Bible itself has to say!

Authority and Perspective

D o you believe that the Bible is inerrant?" the young man with the tape recorder asked.

There was a hush in the audience, for much more than a theological issue was at stake. The setting was the lecture hall at a seminary in Latin America. This particular seminary has done much for the cause of theological education, not only in its own denomination and geographical setting, but throughout Latin America and for several denominations. Much of its funding came from the United States, from a denomination that had recently been taken over by a rabidly fundamentalist faction. The faculty and administration had taken a risk in inviting me to lecture, for they knew that they were under serious scrutiny by some who wanted their funding to be discontinued. In consequence, I had been very careful to stick to church history, and to avoid any subject that might put the existence of the seminary in jeopardy. I had been particularly careful not to say a word about the Bible or its historical accuracy. But the young man with the tape recorder had been sent by representatives of the fundamentalist faction in the denomination, to check on what was being taught at the seminary. When the floor was opened for questions from the audience he saw his opportunity. I even imagined that I saw a glint of triumph in his eyes as he stood up with his tape recorder and asked: "Do you believe that the Bible is inerrant?"

Finally, after a moment of hushed expectation, I responded, "Yes! The Bible is inerrant. But the same cannot be said for any interpretation of the Bible. The error is not in the Bible, but in its interpreters, who often confuse their own words with the Word of God."

"What do you mean? Can you give me an example?"

"Surely. As a matter of fact, I'll give you two. In John 15:1, Jesus says that he is 'the true vine.' If I were to tell you that this means that Jesus has roots, and a trunk, and leaves, and needs dirt and fertilizer in order to live, you probably would say that I was mistaken. Jesus is not really and literally a vine. The text must be interpreted in some other fashion. You probably would say that the text is an allegory, that its language is metaphoric. Yet the text itself does not say that it is an allegory or a metaphor. There is no error in the text. The error would be in the interpreter who takes it literally when it is not intended to be literal. Isn't that so?" I asked, as he nodded in agreement. Then I continued: "Now, then, in Genesis 1 we are told that God made the world in six days. Just as in the case of John 15, the text does not tell us whether we are to interpret it literally or not. If you insist that the text must be taken literally, that is your privilege, and there certainly is nothing in the text to contradict you. But there is also nothing in the text that says that it must be taken literally. Therefore your position, as well as the position of someone who says that text is to be taken as a metaphor, is based, not on the text itself, but on your interpretation of the text. If either you or that other person err, the error is not in the text itself, but in its interpretation. That is why I say that the Bible is inerrant, but the same cannot be said for any interpretation of the Bible. As a matter of fact, for me to claim that my interpretation is inerrant is to usurp the authority of the Bible. And the same is true of any interpretation, no matter whether literal or metaphorical."

At that point, the young man sat down and turned off his tape recorder. I looked at the president of the seminary, who winked at me and sighed in relief.

Obviously, there was some sleight of hand in that argument. Inerrancy, as I defined it in that discussion, can be claimed with equal grounds for any text, for in the final analysis it is not texts that err, but their interpreters. If the young man had been quicker of wit, and had asked me, "Does that mean that the plays of Shakespeare or of Lope de Vega are inerrant?" I would have been forced to answer "Yes," and my entire argument would have come tumbling down.

Yet the point remains—for the Bible as well as for Lope de Vega—that no reading of a text is completely and absolutely corroborated by the text itself. Reading is always a dialogue between the text and the reader. It is not only the text that speaks and the reader who listens, but also the reader who asks questions of the text, and the text responds.

There is a poetically mysterious dimension to any dialogue.[1] How is it that I, a center of being and consciousness that no one can fully understand—not even myself—can express my thoughts and sentiments in words that are themselves subject to interpretation, and hope to communicate with another center of being that is fully as mysterious as myself? When I say "God is love," my understanding of "God," of "love," and even of "is," is shaded and nuanced by myriad experiences, many of which I do not understand nor even suspect. The same is true of the person who hears my words. And yet, I believe—and I know—that dialogue is possible. Somehow, it is worthwhile to say to another "God is love," even though our understanding of those words will never be exactly the same. Dialogue, mysterious and seemingly impossible though it might be, is the basis of our entire social life. It is the hope that communication might be possible that sustains me as I make a phone call, preach a sermon, or write a book. You, my reader, will certainly not read this book exactly as I intended it. Yet I persist in writing it presuming on the poetically mysterious miracle of dialogue, whereby, in spite of its impossibility, communication does take place.

When the miracle of dialogue really happens, the otherness of each party is respected; what one party says is not to be understood merely on the basis of the whims of the other. I must not allow myself to hear you saying whatever I please, whatever fits my presuppositions.

Your words have a normative dimension that I must not violate. On the other hand, I can only hear them within my context and from my own perspective. And yet, dialogue takes place, and somehow we manage to communicate. Communication is that mysterious bridge where intimacy and otherness meet.

To read the Bible is to enter into dialogue with it. In that dialogue, there is a sense in which the text is normative, just as the interlocutor of any other dialogue is normative. Impossible though the task may be, I must strive to understand the ancient text in its own context. I know that I cannot jump back to the time of the Exile in Babylon, nor even to the time of the Roman Empire—living late in the twentieth century is difficult enough! No matter how much I study the original languages, I shall never understand the nuances of every turn of phrase the way a native speaker would have understood them. And yet I must take the text and its context in all seriousness. That is why the study of the biblical languages and of all the disciplines, which in various ways contribute to the historico-critical method, is so important. I must listen to the text as I would to another, respecting and trying to understand its otherness.

At the same time, the other pole of the dialogue is just as important. It is I, from my context and my perspective, who read the text. In order for there to be true dialogue, the text must engage me, not as I would be had I lived at the time of the Babylonian exile, but as I am here and now. It is not only the text that speaks to me, but I who speak to the text, demanding its responses in genuine dialogue.

Had the young man with the tape recorder asked me about Lope de Vega, I probably would have responded along the lines of these two poles of any dialogue with a text. First of all, I would have said that the question is not one of inerrancy, but rather one of authority. Texts do not err. It is writers and readers who err. But texts do have authority, and therefore the question is: How is the authority of the Bible different from that of Lope de Vega's plays? Obviously, at an initial level, their authority differs in that it refers to different matters. Only a very confused person would go to the Bible in preference to Lope de Vega in order to learn about Spanish life at the end of the fifteenth century and the beginning of the sixteenth. But the difference is much greater than that. The authority of the Bible is grounded on both ends of our dialogue with the biblical text. The Bible is authoritative both because we, its interlocutors, grant it authority, and because throughout the life of the church it has proven itself worthy of that authority—in other words, because when we enter into a dialogue with it, it responds with authority. This authority is not "objective" in the sense that it can be proven to all comers, no matter what their religious or philosophical stance. Nor is it "subjective" in the sense that it depends upon my granting it authority. It is rather dialogical. The Bible is authoritative because, when the church addresses it, it addresses the church with authority.

In the foregoing, I have often referred to the perspective of the interpreter. The question of perspective is important for two complementary reasons: first, because it cannot be avoided; second, because it should not be avoided.

First, perspective cannot be avoided. If there is anything we have learned during these last decades of modernity, it is that knowledge is always perspectival. We probably would have learned it much sooner had we really listened to Immanuel Kant, who showed that objective knowledge is a contradiction in terms. But the modern age was so enamored with the dream of objectivity that it has taken us two centuries to begin to understand the implications of what Kant was telling us. Kicking and screaming, shaken and poked by the likes of Freud and Marx, modernity has finally begun to awaken from its dream of objectivity, and the result has been the birth of postmodernity. (In a way, much of what I say here is based on the postmodern critique of modernity's false sense of objectivity—or, in more technical terms, of the great modern metanarrative—for it is precisely that critique that leads to an insistence on the importance of perspective in any claim to knowledge. Yet, in some ways what I say here, rather than "postmodern," hopes to express some of the "extramodern" experience of a community that was largely excluded from modernity—or rather, that was included as an object rather than as a subject.)[2]

Precisely because perspective cannot be avoided, when it is not explicitly acknowledged the result is that a particular perspective takes on an aura of universality. Thus it happens that theology from a male perspective claims to be generally human, and that North Atlantic white theology believes itself to be "normal," while theologies from the so-called Third World or from ethnic minorities in the North Atlantic are taken to be contextual or perspectival.

Just as important for our purposes is the second point, namely, that the matter of perspective should not be avoided. The reason for this is not simply that we delude ourselves when we believe that ours is not a particular perspective. The reason is rather that, unless the text addresses us where we are, it does not really address us. If a black woman in Africa reads a biblical text in exactly the same way in which she was taught to read it by a white man from Nebraska, the text will most likely be addressing issues that were important for her teacher and for other white men in Nebraska, but will not be addressing other issues that relate more directly to that woman's life. If I do not speak to the text, asking of it questions that are genuinely my own, the text will not really speak to me, and the dialogue will be undercut.

Perspective, however, does not mean fragmentation. Whenever one speaks of theology being contextual, there are those who raise the question of the possibility that the contextualization of theology may lead to the fragmentation of the church. This is a legitimate concern, and one that must be addressed, for history shows that contextualization may indeed lead to divisiveness. Such was, for instance, the principal root of the long-standing schism between the Latin West and the Greek East. Over the centuries, each of these two branches of the church contextualized the gospel in its own culture, and the time came when each accused the other of heresy. To say, however, that contextualization is what led to schism is to miss an important distinction. What led to schism was not contextualization itself, but *unconscious* contextualization. The inculturation of the gospel in the Greek-speaking East was a positive and necessary result of the evangelization of the East. And the inculturation of the gospel in the Latin-speaking West was also a positive and necessary result of the evangelization of the West. The problem lay in that neither the Greek-speaking East nor the Latin-speaking West was willing or able to acknowledge that its own understanding and expression of the

16

gospel were contextual. On the contrary, each of them insisted that its own theology was nothing but "the faith once delivered to the apostles." On that basis, there was no option left but to reject and condemn all different understandings of any aspects of the faith, as well as any practice of the faith that did not agree with one's own. Precisely because contextualization had taken place, but was not acknowledged, contextualization resulted in schism.

The same is true today. Contextualization may certainly lead to fragmentation; but that is not necessarily its result. *Unconscious* contextualization, on the other hand, will certainly lead to fragmentation, because it is by nature sectarian, not recognizing that it is but part of the whole. What leads to fragmentation is not the existence of a black theology, a Hispanic[3] theology, or theologies that explicitly take into account the theologian's gender. What leads to fragmentation is the lack of recognition that all these theologies, as well as all expressions of traditional theology, are contextual, and therefore express the gospel as seen from a particular perspective. None of them can claim to speak for the whole. Any theology that claims universality is by definition sectarian and divisive—even if it is what the church has traditionally taken as normative and universal.

It is for these reasons that I prefer to speak of "perspectives" in theology. It is not a matter of each particular group having its own truth, quite apart from all the rest. On that basis, since any group can be further subdivided, we would come to the conclusion that truth in theology is a purely individual matter, and would thus fall into a radical solipsism in which no dialogue is possible.

To speak of "perspectives" is to imagine that we are all looking at a landscape. The landscape itself is the same for all of us. Yet each one sees it from a different perspective, and will thus describe it differently. Since we are dealing with the interpretation of the Scripture, it may be well to spell out some of the implications of this image of a landscape with a multitude of observers.

First of all, it is important to remember that we are all looking at the same landscape. We may certainly see it in myriad different ways; but we still are all speaking of a single landscape, of a common text. This is part of what binds us together. The primary subject of our conversation is not our varying perspectives, important as they are. Our conversation is about the landscape, and how it is illumined from each of our various vantage points. This means that, although what we seek here is an interpretation of the Bible as seen through Hispanic eyes, it is still an interpretation *of the Bible,* and not simply of our experiences, good or bad.

Second, although we are speaking primarily of the landscape, we do not stand as outsiders to it. We are not outside observers, as if we were watching a movie. We stand within the landscape. We are affected by the landscape. Since we are people of faith, we can even say that we are defined by the landscape. We are also part of the view that other observers see, from their own perspective. And they too are part of the total landscape that we see. Part of the beauty of a landscape is that it draws me, the observer, into it, so that I am engulfed and in a way defined by its greatness. In the case of biblical interpretation, we are people who stand in faith, who believe that the Bible speaks to us, and who therefore are quite conscious that what we are describing is not simply a landscape "out there," but rather something that is at the very heart of our lives. We are not speaking of the biblical text as if it were dead letter, ancient history, distant memories. We are speaking of a text in which we find ourselves, our very lives.

Third, as in the case of a landscape, it is absolutely impossible for two people to stand at exactly the same place at the same time. Some will stand so close to each other that their views will be virtually indistinguishable. Others, standing at a greater distance, will have widely differing perspectives. This means that, while it will be possible to classify various perspectives, all such classifications will be provisional, and may shift according to the issue at hand. We may say, for instance, that there is a group of people looking at a landscape from hill A, others from hill B, and still others from the bottom of the valley. Generally speaking, those on hill A will share a common perspective, which will be distinguishable from those on hill B. Yet there will be among those on hill A some who are on top of the hill, others who are lower down the slope, some who are standing to the right, others who are sitting to the left, some who are looking at the horizon, others who are more interested on the river at the bottom of the valley, and so on. Thus, those who share the common perspective of hill A could also be divided into various subgroups, according to a variety of criteria. Likewise, when we speak of "a Hispanic perspective," we must immediately acknowledge that this is just one of many possible ways of classifying perspectives, and that even among Latinos there is a wide variety of perspectives. There are Hispanic males and females, poor, rich, and in between, liberals and conservatives, young and old, Puerto Ricans, Chicanos, and others. This is why, in a conversation such as this, we are always tempted to spend so much time trying to define who we are—what our common perspective is—that we never get to look at the landscape itself. The only way to move beyond such an impasse is to speak of "*a* Hispanic perspective," making an effort to be as inclusive as possible and hoping that such a perspective resonates with other Hispanics, but knowing that it must never claim to be *the* Hispanic perspective.

At the same time, it is important to remember that Latinos stand together with many others who speak out of similar experiences of marginalization, suffering, and poverty. While we must learn to read the Bible through our own eyes, we must constantly stand in solidarity with those who, out of similar experiences, read it in a similar fashion. From them we have much to learn. To them—and to the church at large—we offer the insights of our perspective, as resources for our common struggles.

Fourth, a variety of perspectives enriches everyone's appreciation of the landscape itself. If I stand on hill A, someone from hill B can point out features in the landscape that I would never have noticed on my own. If I am interested in the way light bounces off of rocks and rivers, I can contribute something to my neighbor, whose interest lies in the various shades of green in the forest below us. Through conversation, we can amplify each other's experience of the landscape—and thereby we can enhance each other's lives. Thus, I affirm my own perspective, not in order to claim that it is only I who understand the landscape, but rather in order to enrich the entire community of observers around me. And I am also much impoverished if I do not listen to what they have to say about the landscape as they see it from their own unique perspectives.

Finally, and most important, all of this is worth doing only because we believe in the miracle of communication. Thanks to communication, I do not stand alone in the landscape. Thanks to communication, those others who stand with and around me, both near and far, are much more than silent features in the landscape. They address me in their otherness. They speak to me, both of themselves and of their own vistas as they look at the landscape. They enrich my enjoyment of the landscape, forcing me to move around, to shift into their perspectives, to see the towering rock or the small bush I had missed. Some of the great landscape artists owe their greatness precisely to their ability to present in a single picture a vista that is subtly yet coherently enriched by a variety of perspectives. Likewise, our interpretation of the biblical text will be enhanced as we take into account the variety of perspectives offered to us by the entire church catholic.

Such a variety of perspectives is not only valuable; it is absolutely necessary. Although in the preceding paragraph I have used words such as "enhancing" and "enriching," we are not dealing here with an optional enhancement to Christian theology—like chrome trimming on an automobile. We are dealing rather with something that belongs to the very nature of the church, and without which the church cannot be true to its own nature—more like the four wheels on a car. To say that the church is "catholic" means that it includes within itself a variety of perspectives.[4] To say that it is "one" means that such multiplicity, rather than dividing it, brings it closer together. This is the miracle of communication, which in Christian theology we ascribe to the Holy Spirit.

Significantly, in the book of Acts the first consequence of the outpouring of the Holy Spirit on the disciples—men and women, the Twelve as well as the others—is their ability to communicate. Thanks to the Spirit, these disciples can communicate with a variety of peoples; and their communication is not centripetal or imperialistic. The Spirit does not impose on all the language of the original disciples, but rather makes it possible for various people to understand "each in their own native language." From the very outset, the

Spirit makes the church truly catholic by including in it a variety of languages and cultural perspectives—even though, as the rest of the book of Acts and the entire history of the church show, on this score Christians have constantly and repeatedly resisted the Spirit.

Thus, if I dare offer to the church at large these reflections on "the Bible through Hispanic eyes," it is first of all trusting in the Spirit of God, who will create communication while respecting our differences, and build intimacy while affirming our distinct identities. And it is also trusting that the Spirit, who enriched the church with Elamites, Parthians, Cappadocians, Greeks, Anglo-Saxons, and all the rest, will also see fit to enrich the church and its understanding of the Scripture with the gifts and perspectives that we Latinos offer to the whole.

An Autobiographical Note

If perspective is as important as I have said above, it seems necessary that I give the reader a clearer indication of the particular perspective from which I read the Scripture, and how I have reached it.

I grew up as a Protestant (Methodist) in a country (Cuba) where most of my neighbors were at least nominally Roman Catholic. This was long before the Second Vatican Council, and therefore the prejudices and misunderstandings on both sides were even greater than they are now—and they certainly are still enormous. My more devout Catholic classmates crossed themselves, almost as in an exorcism, when I told them that I was a Protestant. Some assured me that Protestants do not believe in God or in Jesus, and therefore cannot go to heaven. I for my part was no less prejudiced. Catholics were idolaters who worshiped the saints instead of God and who put Mary in the place of Jesus. An important part of my task as a Christian was to convert Catholics from their errors, and "bring them to Christ."

One thing that clearly distinguished us Protestants in those days and in that setting was the Bible. On Sundays, one could always recognize a "sister" or a "brother" from another church, because they carried a Bible. On Wednesdays, we gathered for Bible study. During the rest of the week, we often debated with Catholics on the basis of the Bible. Indeed, a favorite sport of some of us in the youth group was to spot a priest or a nun and engage them in a debate. And, partly as a preparation for that sport and partly out of profound devotion, we read the Bible religiously. Three times I read it from cover to cover during my teen years.

Yet, there was a difference between my reading of the Bible at that time and what I have later come to know as a fundamentalist reading. Fundamentalism is a reaction to the doubts about Scripture raised by modernity—as many fundamentalists would say, against "modernism." As a result, it too is a modern reading of the Bible. It seeks in the sacred page objective information of the same sort that modernity seeks in a laboratory or a telescope. In contrast, my reading of the Bible was premodern. Even when I was aware of some of the doubts raised by modernity, I felt free simply to ignore them. They were not my issues. My issues were how to confound and convert Catholics and nonbelievers—which were almost the same—and how to live a fuller Christian life. The fundamentalists I knew as I was growing up often read the Bible with anger, almost as if they cherished the damnation of the rest of the world. Most often, I would read it with joy, because it was a guide and a friend. I would read it seeking after wisdom, rather than mere information. I would read it for its beauty, as poetry, and therefore had no difficulty when my professors told me that the earth took eons to create, or that humanity was the result of a long process of evolution. It was sometimes obscure and unintelligible, but most often a life-giving text.

Since I was never a fundamentalist, even when my reading of the Scripture was precritical, I have often argued that most Hispanic Protestants are not fundamentalists, even though from the perspective of those brought up in the liberal tradition and the historico-critical method they might seem to be such. Fundamentalism is a militant response to the challenges of modernity. My reading of the Scripture was—and for most Latino Protestants still is—precritical, and even naive, but not fundamentalist.

This is also the reason why I resonate to the words of the Rev.

Edgar Avitia, one of the participants in our dialogue on the Bible, when he said, *¡Ha sido tan buena la Biblia con nosotros!* ("The Bible has been so good to us!") He said it with a tone of grateful tenderness that reminded me of a child speaking of its mother. He said it as someone who had lived through experiences similar to those I have just described. He said it as I too would wish to say it.

Then I went to seminary (still in Cuba), and immediately new vistas opened before me. I was introduced to the historico-critical method of Bible study. I learned to distinguish among different levels of redaction, and to place texts in their historical setting. It was a fascinating experience, for now I understood much in the Bible that I did not understand before. For a time, I was so fascinated with the new methods and vistas, that I was convinced that, by simply following those methods, the Bible would become much more relevant for my life and for the life of the church.

The result, however, was not as I had expected. By a process so subtle and so slow that I was not aware of it until long after it had taken place, I came to a point where I could understand the Bible much better than before, but no longer had any idea what to do with it. To teach the Bible became synonymous with explaining the historical setting of texts, and the process by which they had been redacted and transmitted. I remember a series of Bible studies on 1 Corinthians that I led in the church where I was working as a senior in seminary. It was an excellent course on the composition of the epistle, on where Paul was when he wrote it, and on its relationship to the rest of the Corinthian correspondence. I was able to impart much information, but was able to draw little wisdom from the epistle itself. Also, my Bible study lacked the engagement I had experienced in our Bible studies years earlier, when we read Paul, not primarily to learn about the life of the church in Corinth, but to learn what it meant to be the church in our own day. Even more tragically, I came to realize that my Bible study, far from making the Bible more accessible to the people, made it more distant, for now they could do nothing with it unless a more learned person told them all there was to know on issues of dating, authorship, and composition.

Years later, I discovered that many others, from different perspectives and life stories, were coming to similar conclusions. I was even pleased and encouraged to find similar sentiments in scholars who had been carefully trained in the historico-critical methods. Thus, I find myself agreeing with Sandra M. Schneiders, of the Jesuit School of Theology at Berkeley:

> Against a background of profound respect, indeed, admiration, for the prodigious accomplishments of modern historical critical biblical scholarship, this conclusion is nevertheless critical, even harsh: contemporary New Testament scholarship actually lacks a developed hermeneutical theory. To that extent, it does not really "know what it is doing" in the theoretical sense of that expression. It knows *how* to do what it is doing, but has uncritically taken for granted that *what* it is doing is exactly and only what needs to be done in order for this text, which is probably still the most influential text in the Western world, to be truly understood.[5]

Something similar happened to my preaching. I knew how to do the exegesis of a text, but had no idea what to do with the exegesis itself. The most widely used commentary among my classmates, and the one that my professors recommended, was *The Interpreter's Bible,* in which the exegesis of a text was done by one author, and the exposition by another, apparently without any relationship between the two. Therefore my preaching, often modeled after that commentary, and other times simply out of desperation, became moral exhortations in which the biblical text was at best a pretext for what I would have said anyhow.

Theologically, the seminary where I studied drew its inspiration mainly from Karl Barth and neo-orthodoxy. This was helpful, for Barth had much to say about the Word of God and its power and authority. In some ways, he seemed to be expressing a joy in the Word similar to what my classmates and I had in our earlier lives as Christians. Thus, I had no difficulty accepting that theology and making it mine. The problem was that those who taught me how to study the Bible drew their inspiration elsewhere, from the liberal tradition and from the historico-critical method, which moved along parallel lines like a team of yoked oxen. The result, again, was that I could preach excellent theological sermons, but had only a very vague idea how to relate them to the Scriptures that I myself declared to be authoritative.

This in turn had two other consequences. The first was that, just as my Bible studies, my preaching did not bring the Scripture closer to the people, but farther away. My preaching was generally biblical, in that it dealt with some of the basic teachings of the Scripture. But, since its real starting point was not the Bible, but theology, it taught by implication that the Bible is not really accessible to the people, who need to have a theological education before they can read it and understand its significance for their lives. My preaching, like my Bible study, while claiming to take the Bible to the people, actually built a fence around the Bible—a fence as high as any that existed in the worst times of the much-maligned Middle Ages.

The second consequence was that the whole issue of the authority of the Bible was a matter of much mystification for me, as well as for those whom I presumed to teach. I insisted on the authority of the Bible because that was one of the principles of the Reformation, because neo-orthodoxy also claimed it, and even in some vague way because in earlier years the Bible had been good to me. But it was really a nonfunctioning authority. In truth, authority lay in theology, in religious experience, and even in religious and moral platitudes, and the Bible functioned only insofar as what it said agreed with these other authorities.

In many ways, these were the dry years. They were productive in attainments and in scholarship. I devoted myself to the study of historical theology, received a doctorate in that field, and published extensively in it. I taught in prestigious seminaries, first in Puerto Rico, and then in the United States. Still, this was a time that St. John of the Cross would have called *noche oscura del alma*—the dark night of the soul. It was not a matter of an overwhelming sense of sin, as it had been for Augustine, for Luther, and for Ignatius. It was rather a matter of a dysfunction between theology and practice, between what I said and even believed regarding the authority of the Scripture, and the way the Scripture actually functioned in my life and in my teaching and theology. I kept on speaking and teaching as if the Bible had authority; but I did not see that authority functioning firsthand. At that point, my feelings were what I suppose must have been also Wesley's as he followed Peter Böler's advice: "Preach faith till you have it; and then, because you have it, you will preach faith."

The way out did not come through an Aldersgate-like experience,[6] although it did produce a strange warming of the heart. It came through a series of circumstances and encounters in the late sixties and throughout the seventies.

First among these was the new theology coming from Roman Catholics in Latin America. I was living in Puerto Rico, and traveling regularly throughout Central and South America, at the time of the Second Vatican Council, and had the opportunity to witness some of the significant changes that were taking place among those Roman Catholics whom as a youth I had discounted as idolaters. The mass was translated into the vernacular and set to native tunes and rhythms. There were ecumenical gatherings and conversations galore. *Liberation theology* became almost a household term, with books in Spanish and Portuguese becoming overnight theological bestsellers. Although I read and appreciated many of these books, and they certainly impacted my theological outlook, for me the most important development taking place in Latin America was that people began to gather in small groups to read and study the Bible. These were the same sort of people whom years earlier I had challenged to conversion, Bible in hand. But they were now claiming the Bible as their own, not as a tool for anti-Protestant polemics, but rather as a light unto their path. People who had a general knowledge of the biblical narrative, but who had never read the Bible itself, began to read it and to act upon it. Since they had no idea what they were supposed to find in a particular text, they often found things no one expected. They began sharing their findings, first orally, then in mimeographed sheets, and some eventually in printed form. What I read in those reports, and what I heard when I had the opportunity to listen in on such gatherings, brought new life to the Bible. The Bible was good to them! And, partly through their influence, the Bible was once again good to me!

Another parallel occurrence, with similar consequences, was the development of women's theology both in the United States and abroad. Some of the women discounted the Bible as outright oppressive. Although I tried to understand—and, to the degree that such a thing is possible, did understand—the reasons and the depth of their anger, they were not particularly helpful in bringing the Bible back to life. But there were other women who struggled with the Scriptures and with its traditional interpretations, with the conviction that the Bible could and should be interpreted differently, and would thus support rather than hinder the liberation of women. One such woman was Catherine Gunsalus, who later became my wife. Shortly after we were married, we were asked by the Presbyterian Church (U.S.) to write a study book on women in the Bible who did new things.[7] It was a most rewarding experience. The Bible had been good to Catherine! And, partly through her influence, the Bible was once again good to me!

This was also the time when, in my own inner identity, I began to move from being a Latin American living temporarily in the United States to being a Hispanic in the United States. I traveled throughout the United States, meeting Latinos in various regions and denominations, sometimes speaking or preaching to them, but many other times listening to what they had to say. I visited national Hispanic conventions of several denominations. I worshiped in Pentecostal churches in Los Angeles and Episcopal churches in the Bronx. I joined the Hispanic Instructors group at Perkins School of Theology, and taught brief courses for Hispanics there and in several other seminaries. I joined the Río Grande Conference—a United Methodist annual conference primarily serving the Hispanic population of Texas and New Mexico. In all these settings I met and heard people who interpreted the Bible in ways that were radically relevant to their situation, and also in ways that were refreshing and liberating. The Bible was good to them! And, partly through their influence, the Bible was once again good to me!

Which Hispanic Eyes?

The very fact that I have gone through the various stages described above should serve as a warning that there is no such thing as *the*

Latino perspective on the Bible—or on anything else, for that matter. There are many Hispanics— probably the majority—who continue to interpret the Bible in the naively joyous, precritical way in which I read it when I was a teenager. (A type of reading which, at least in part, can find vindication in some of the postmodern critiques of modernity and its presuppositions.) There are others—mostly in the so-called mainline denominations—who are still caught in the dilemma in which I was when I finished my schooling, not knowing what to do with the Bible, and yet convinced they must do something with it. And there are still others—a rapidly growing number—for whom the Bible is good once more, because it speaks directly to their struggles and hopes.

When the Hispanic Instructors at Perkins were discussing the project that resulted in this book, it was clear to all of us that this would not be simply a compilation of all sorts of Latino interpretations of the Bible. Saúl Trinidad, a pastor from Detroit, told of a Latino church that uses Deuteronomy 22:5 to ban women who wear pants—even though when that passage was written neither men nor women wore pants! Others mentioned the growing influx of dispensationalist interpretations, where the Bible is read in order to discover what prophecies are being fulfilled in our day, and what will happen next—even though similar interpretations have been offered through the centuries, and not one of them has been right! In conclusion, said the Reverend Trinidad, "The fact that I am Hispanic (or rather *mestizo*) is no guarantee that my reading will be through Hispanic eyes."

In those words, Trinidad was using the phrase "through Hispanic eyes" in a narrower sense than simply through any Hispanic eyes. In a literal sense, Hispanic eyes are those that read Deuteronomy 22:5 as a prohibition against women wearing pants. And Hispanic eyes are also those that read the passages about the beast in Revelation as referring to the European Common Market. Yet that is not what we mean by "Hispanic eyes" in this context.

What we mean by "Hispanic eyes" is the perspective of those who claim their Hispanic identity as part of their hermeneutical baggage, and who also read the Scripture within the context of a commitment to the Latino struggle to become all that God wants us and all of the world to be—in other words, the struggle for salvation/liberation.

In this context, the story of Moses is instructive. Hebrews hits the nail on the head: "By faith Moses, when he was grown up, refused to be called a son of Pharaoh's daughter, choosing rather to share ill-treatment with the people of God . . ." (Heb. 11:24-25). Like Moses, a growing number of Hispanics can share in the wealth, comfort, and prestige of the NorthAmerican mainstream. Most of the Hispanic Instructors who were participating in this exercise are among that number. Yet, we also know that there is an even greater and faster growing number of Hispanics who live below the poverty line, with little or no educational opportunities, inadequate housing, and slight reward for their work and their efforts. The culture and traditions that we all share are constantly devalued by the dominant culture, and by its expression in the media and in academic circles. Those of us who do not live under the harsh conditions of other Latinos are constantly tempted to distance ourselves from them. It would not be difficult to do so, for thanks to our education—and, in the case of the Hispanic Instructors, our ecclesiastical connections— we could easily pass for children of the daughter of Pharaoh. But, as Trinidad pointed out, "There is a point at which we have to take hold of our own identity. Only then can we really read the Bible through Hispanic eyes. It is not only a matter of leaving aside the comforts of life, but rather an option of consciousness and of identity." This is never an easy matter, and most often is not planned. Again, at this point it may be well to remember the story of Moses, who opts for the children of Israel, not out of a considered decision, but simply out of a reaction against the injustice of an Egyptian overseer, and who then goes through a long period of exile before that option comes to fruition in the vision of the burning bush.

Such are the "Hispanic eyes" through which we intend to read the Bible in the pages that follow.

Finally, a further word of clarification. Obviously, much of what Hispanic eyes see is what most other eyes see. Returning once again to the simile of a landscape and many observers from different perspectives, if at the center of the landscape there is a river, it is most likely that most observers, no matter what their perspective, will see the river. They will all have this in common, as something that binds them together. Yet, when speaking of their different perspectives they will speak not so much of the river itself, but of the various ways the river and the rest of the landscape appear from their particular standpoints. One will talk of the sun glistening on the river. Another of the palm trees reflected on the water. Still another of the contrasting colors of the water. This does not mean that there is no river in common. It means simply that, when speaking of varying perspectives, it is the differences that stand out. Likewise, when speaking of "the Bible through Hispanic eyes" there is much that such eyes will see that will coincide with what Christians have seen throughout the ages. Indeed, much of what the Hispanic Instructors read and heard in the process of this project was no different than what they would have read and heard in other Christian contexts. Yet that is not noted here, for our purpose is to explore and to show what "Hispanic eyes" or a Latino perspective can contribute to the understanding of the Scripture, not only on the part of Hispanics, but also of those others who, albeit from different perspectives, share the same landscape and the same faith with us.

CHAPTER ONE

Marginality

Not all Latinos have the same experience, and therefore not all readings "through Hispanic eyes" are alike. There are differences of gender—differences that are quite crucial in communities where males often suppress their own consciousness of oppression by oppressing females. There are differences of origin—differences that sometimes are overplayed by those in the dominant culture who wish to justify their unresponsiveness on the basis of our own divisiveness, but which nevertheless are quite real. Some of us are descendants of the original inhabitants of these lands, who were here long before the arrival of the first Europeans. Some of us are descendants of African slaves brought to work for Spanish masters. Some of us are descendants of the Spanish conquistadors and colonizers. Most of us are a mixture of these and other strains. In background, some of us are Mexican, others Puerto Rican, others Cuban, or Dominican, or Central American. Some can claim more than one of these various backgrounds. Some of us were born in the United States. Others came as political exiles. Still others came for economic and other reasons. Many of us are not even quite sure why we are here. Some call ourselves "Latino/as," others "Hispanics," or

"Hispanic-Americans." Some prefer more concrete identifications: "Chicano," "Puerto Rican," "Cuban-American," "Mexican-American," "Salvadoran," and so on.

With such a variety of experiences and backgrounds, it is not surprising that there is no one hermeneutical paradigm that fits all of us. Perhaps one could even go so far as to claim that there is no one hermeneutical paradigm that fits any of us! At various times and situations, most of us would prefer one paradigm over another. Therefore, rather than trying to offer a single perspective or a single clue to a "reading with Hispanic eyes," I have decided to organize what follows around five paradigms or perspectives that Latinos employ when reading both the Bible and their own situation. Clearly, this classification, like any taxonomy of living organisms, is somewhat arbitrary. At various points, these different paradigms overlap, or two of them are applied simultaneously to the same text. Still, I believe that our discussion of Hispanic hermeneutics will be enriched and made more understandable by organizing it around these five themes or paradigms, and devoting a chapter to each.

The first such paradigm or perspective is *marginality*. No matter what our background, most Latinos, when speaking of their own experience in this society and in the church within this society, identify with the image of marginality.

This became quite clear to me some fifteen years ago, when a group of us was planning a journal on Hispanic theology. We knew what we wanted: a journal that would reread the Bible, theology, and history from our own perspective(s); one that would bring together the concerns and experiences of Chicanos, Puerto Ricans, and all others who call themselves "Hispanics" or "Latinos." But we did not know what to call it, or what to use as a theme or logo on the cover. We toyed with dozens of names and logos. Someone suggested Don Quixote charging at a church that looked like a windmill. But others objected that this was too Spanish, and did not take into account the native background that is also part of who we are. Someone else suggested a Mexican hat and a guitar. But it immediately became clear that this left out the African background of many of us. One after another, all proposals were turned down as not being sufficiently inclusive.

Then someone suggested the name *Apuntes,* and the subtitle: *Reflexiones desde el margen hispano*—Reflections from the Hispanic Margin. The suggestion was immediately received as one that really brought all of us together. *Apuntes* had the value of being a somewhat ambiguous word which could be taken to mean "jottings" but also "aimings." Thus, this title would allow us to consider ourselves as merely making marginal jottings at the edge of theology, but also as aiming at some core issues within church and theology. Note that a common denominator of both meanings is that in both cases one stands outside the center, either making marginal notes or taking aim at something in the center. At that point, the question of what to use for a cover was easily answered. We would take a page from a classical Christian author, and write marginal notes to it. On this we all happily agreed, and adjourned the meeting in order to celebrate what we were convinced was an inspired solution to our dilemma.

The point was clear. While we sought to define our own identity by means of a central theme or logo, we could not do it. Clearly, there is something—or rather, several somethings—at the core of our being that bind us together: language, culture, history, traditions. But all of these are sufficiently varied that when we try to pin them down they prove both unitive and divisive. The one point at which there is a commonality of experience and perspective is marginality.

As we speak of marginality, it is important to recognize that this is a convenient image to describe a fairly complex situation. To be marginal means to be excluded from the center. That is an experience with which most Latinos identify. Yet, the notion of marginality must be nuanced in two ways. First, since we live in a polycentric society, most of us stand at the margin in some relationships, and at the center in others. As Hispanics, we stand at the margin of the dominant cultural and political trends in our society. Yet those of us who are educated, or male, or wealthy stand at the center in other relationships. Second, marginality is not always entirely imposed. Many Christians in the early church remained marginal to the affairs of their society because fuller participation would have involved them in idolatry and immorality. Likewise, Hispanics and other cultural minorities often feel the need to make a space for themselves and their culture—a space at the margins of society, and yet a space in which we can be ourselves in ways we cannot be when totally immersed in the dominant culture. Thus, the marginality imposed from outside is often reinforced by a self-created marginalization.

In any case, as the group of Hispanic Instructors collected our biblical reflections, it was clear that this perspective of marginality was a guiding principle in much of our interpretation of texts.

There are many reasons for this, but they can generally be collected under two headings. The first is our experience as Protestants in a culture where the majority are Roman Catholic. In many Latino circles, the new openness and dialogue between Protestants and Catholics that developed after the Second Vatican Council has lagged far behind. This has to do in part with the attitude of many Roman Catholics who feel that Hispanics should by rights be Catholics, and that therefore Hispanic Protestants are traitors to their own culture and traditions. It also has to do with the prevailing attitude in many Hispanic Protestant circles that Roman Catholics are not really Christians, and ought to be converted for the sake of their own salvation. Finally, it has to do with the very marginalization of our communities, where ideas and trends that have been circulating in the dominant society for decades are slow to penetrate. In any case, as Protestants our experience is often one of marginalization even in our own Hispanic communities.

Then we are also marginalized in the larger community, where being Protestant is quite acceptable, but our race, our accent, or even our surname is not as acceptable. And this is certainly true of most of our own denominations, many of which boast of their minority memberships, but seldom give such minorities an opportunity for leadership. And, even when such opportunities are given, the polity of most major Protestant denominations is such that it is very difficult for Hispanic congregations, many of which are poor, to be fully enfranchised in the various denominational structures.

All of this adds up to our reading the Bible, so to speak, "from the margin." When we are left out of what goes on around us in the dominant culture, we read the Bible as a source of strength, and often seeking an explanation for our painful experiences. And, when we feel left out of activities in our own communities (or when our own understanding of the gospel and Christian life leads us to exclude ourselves) it is again in the Bible that we find the strength to see us through. No wonder, then, that brother Avitia says that "the Bible has been so good to us!"

One way in which this perspective "from the margin" leads to a different reading of the text is by identifying with characters who in the biblical narrative itself are marginal. Traditionally, Christians have read the story of Abraham's intended sacrifice of Isaac, and have identified with Abraham's anguish, torn between his love for his son on the one hand, and obeying what he takes to be the will of God on the other. Some, still identifying with Abraham, point out that this was the child of God's promise, and that Abraham was now in a conflict of faith, between the God who had promised and given Isaac, and the same God who now demanded Isaac in sacrifice. A few look at the story from the perspective of Isaac, and dwell on his innocence and his trust. But in chapter 2 we shall see a Hispanic interpretation that looks at the story, at least in part, from the perspective of the ram that was actually sacrificed!

Reading "from the margin" also leads us to see things that often go unnoticed by other interpreters. Look for instance at the story of the election of Matthias in Acts 1. In that story, Peter stands up in the midst of the community of believers and makes a speech that in essence says that, since Judas had fallen along the way, someone should be named to take his place. That in itself is interesting, for Jesus had given them no commandment or instruction that his apostles must be twelve. But apparently Peter is a structural conservative who feels that, since they were twelve at the beginning, they must be twelve again, and they must forever be twelve. Then he establishes a set of criteria that this twelfth person must meet: he must be "one of the men who have accompanied us during all the time that the Lord Jesus went in and out among us, beginning from the baptism of John until the day when he was taken up from us" (Acts 1:21-22). When we see such job qualifications, those of us who have long stood at the margin immediately become suspicious, for we know that often these lists of apparently stringent criteria are used to keep power in the hands of the same small group. So in this particular case, following such suspicions, we go back to the gospel of Luke—to the first part of this two-volume series—and immediately discover that Peter is setting up criteria for others that the eleven themselves do not meet! Although this may surprise others, it does not surprise us, for we have seen the same procedure at work more than once, both in the church and in society at large.

Further reflection leads us to wonder whether we have not misunderstood Luke's purpose in including this story here. Most traditional exegetes see Luke as trying to bolster the institution of "the Twelve," and therefore having their number completed as soon as possible. But there is another likely reading. Note that the election of Matthias comes before the events of Pentecost. Jesus had promised the disciples that they would receive the power of the Holy Spirit in order to be witnesses (Acts 1:8). Yet here, without waiting for the promised power, they decide to appoint another to be a witness. Could it not be that Luke, rather than telling us of the great authority of the Twelve, is telling us of the surprising freedom of the Spirit, who is not bound by the decisions of the disciples, but rather is constantly pushing them into new adventures of obedience? In this regard, remember the passage in Acts 6, where the Twelve decide that seven others will be named in order to manage the distribution of relief, and that they will keep for themselves the task of preaching. Almost immediately after his election Stephen, one of the seven, begins to witness and eventually to preach. In fact, the longest sermon in the entire book of Acts is put on the lips of Stephen, who is not even supposed to be preaching! As people who, for all kinds of reasons, have learned the power of subtle and even unperceived irony, we wonder whether some of these stories in Acts may not have ironic overtones, subtly mocking the self-sufficiency and self-assurance of the church and its leaders!

While the suggestion that there may be a touch of irony in Luke's telling of early Christian history may be debatable, there is another point in the same book that is not debatable. This has to do with the tension between "the people" and those who hold the reins of power. Take a concordance and look up the word *people* (in Greek, *laos*) in the early chapters of Acts. You may be surprised that there is no opposition between the followers of Jesus and "the people." On the contrary, "the people" are constantly on the side of the disciples, who have "the goodwill of all *the people*" (2:47). Then, when the beggar was healed at the Temple gate, "all *the people* saw him walking and praising God," and therefore "all *the people* ran together to them in the portico called Solomon's," where Peter "addressed *the people*" (3:9, 11-12). Then, "while Peter and John were speaking to *the people*, **the priests, the captain of the temple, and the Sadducees** came to them, much annoyed because they were teaching *the people*" (4:1-2). "The next day **their rulers, elders, and scribes** assembled in Jerusalem, with **Annas the high priest, Caiaphas, John, and Alexander, and all who were of the high-priestly family**" (4:5-6). When asked to speak to them, Peter makes it clear that he is aware that he is speaking to a double audience: "**Rulers of the people and elders,** . . . let it be known **to all of you,** and *to all the people of* Israel . . ." (4:8-10). Then, the powerful decide to urge the apostles to stop their activities, "to keep it from spreading further among *the people*" (4:17), and they find "no way to punish them because of *the people*" (4:21). The same pattern continues through chapter 6, where many signs and wonders are done among *the people*, and where we are also told of the apostles that "*the people* held them in high esteem" (5:12-13). Again, those who act against the disciples are **the high priest** and **the Sadducees** (that is, the aristocracy), who with **the captain of the temple** and his **police** arrest the apostles again, "but without violence, for they were afraid of being stoned by *the people*" (5:26).

It is in Acts 6:12 that for the first time "the people" join those who oppose the believers. Again, those who are accustomed to an experience of marginality will quite readily see the realism of the story Luke tells. Until the beginning of Acts 6, all the leadership in the nascent church had been "Hebrews"—that is, people from Palestine who spoke the local Aramaic. As Galileans, these particular "Hebrews" were second-class citizens—a matter to which we shall return in another chapter—but so were most of "the people" whom the high priests and the aristocracy held in contempt, and who in turn looked favorably on this crowd of Galileans who dared stand up against the high and mighty. But now, at the beginning of Acts 6, that early Christian community took a momentous and daring step. It appointed seven "Hellenists"—that is, Jews who were more at home in Hellenistic culture and language than in Aramaic, and who therefore were regarded askance by all "good Jews," no matter of what class or social standing. The result was that the church—at least its Hellenistic elements—now lost the support of "the people," and for the first time we are told that those who opposed Stephen and his preaching "stirred up *the people* as well as **the elders and the scribes**" (6:12). In other words, once the church begins to give positions of leadership to those who are even more marginal than "the people," even these common people turn against it.

To add a further note of realism that can readily be understood by those who have experienced marginality, Luke also tells us that those who "stood up and argued with Stephen," and who eventually provoked his martyrdom, were themselves Hellenists—"some of those who belonged to the synagogue of the Freedmen . . . Cyrenians, Alexandrians, and others of those from Cilicia and Asia" (6:9). Logically, one might expect that the fiercest opposition to the Hellenistic Jews who had become Christians would come from the "Hebrews" among Jews, that is, from the most strictly orthodox and exclusivistic. But what in fact happens is that the opposition comes from Hellenistic synagogues, rather than from the most conservative ones. This again is a common experience among marginalized people, who often feel that they must prove themselves, and their relationship to the center, by acting against those who are even more marginal than they are. Thus it happens that among the Latino population some of the staunchest enemies of Hispanic causes are themselves upwardly mobile Latinos. Some of those Hellenistic Jews who belonged to the synagogue of the Freedmen had to prove that they were true Jews by instigating persecution against Stephen and others like him. Likewise, some Latinos feel that they must prove that they are true Americans by dissociating themselves from the barrio and its struggles. As we say in Spanish, *no hay peor cuña que la del mismo palo*—there is no worse wedge than one taken from the same wood. For similar reasons, it is fairly easy to stir up enmity among various minorities—each has been given the impression that it has something to gain by dissociating itself from the others.

Sometimes the very experience and conscience of marginality leads to strange consequences. This is clearly the case with Matthew 5:23-24: "So when you are offering your gift at the altar, if you remember that your brother or sister has something against you, leave your gift there before the altar and go; first be reconciled to your brother or sister, and then come and offer your gift."

This is another of those passages in which our mind and our convenience play games on us. Ever since the first time I remember taking communion, I remember also being told that the passage meant that when one comes to communion one must do so with a spirit of forgiveness. It would not do to come to the altar with hatred in our hearts. And that may well be true; but that is not what the text says.

The text does not say that if we bring our gift before the altar, and there remember that we have something against our brother or our sister, we should forgive them. The text says rather that if we remember that our sister or our brother have something against us, we must go and be reconciled. And that is much more difficult. If it is a matter of how I feel about another, I can easily change that—or at least I can easily fool myself into thinking that I have changed it. I forgive everybody! Now I can come before the altar!

If, on the other hand, the problem is that we remember that another has something against us, then the matter is much more difficult. It is no longer simply a question of inner feelings, of private decision, of quiet forgiveness. It is rather a question of setting aright whatever is wrong.

It is also a matter of recognizing that others may have something against us; and, even more difficult, of recognizing that they may have a reason to have something against us. Our present good intentions are not enough. In a sense, even our present inner repentance is not enough. The injured brother or sister is not merely something in *my* heart, something I can change by willing it away or by feeling sorry for what I have done. They are a physical reality, out there, with which I must deal, and seek to set things aright, if I am to be faithful to the Lord's injunction. Furthermore, in the verses that appear in Matthew just before this passage, those who stand in need of reconciliation are warned to be about it quickly, before the time of judgment arrives. In a sense, it is best to "settle out of court" with our adversaries than to arrive before the Judge unreconciled, since our Judge is vitally interested in reconciliation and forgiveness.

In all of this, marginality and the consciousness thereof have played a strange series of functions. First, they have made me suspicious of an interpretation in which those who most often wrong others if for no other reason than because they can—because they stand at the center, holding the threads of power and control over the marginalized—are left off the hook too easily. All one has to do if one has wronged someone else is to repent before the Lord. The wrong does not have to be righted. The relationship does not have to be leveled. Inner repentance is enough. Second, marginality means that, in any relationship in which I am marginal and another is central, the text does not really refer directly to me. All I can do is to stand at the margin, waiting for the one who has wronged me and others like me to come and offer reconciliation and reparation. There are many other texts that insist that those who have been wronged must be ready to forgive; but this is not one of them. Third, since in spite of the foregoing, this passage reminds me that marginality is relative; that although in terms of racial and ethnic relations in this country I stand at the margins, there are many other contexts and relationships in which I stand at the center, and push others to the margin. As a male, I enjoy privileges and considerations that most women do not enjoy. As a North American citizen, I enjoy rights and an economic status that the vast majority of humankind lacks. In education, income, comfort, and in many other ways, I am not truly marginal. Thus, what my experience of marginality as a Latino allows me to see in those relationships in which I stand at the margin, I must also be willing to see in those other relationships in which I stand at the center. This is why in the Old Testament, particularly in Leviticus and Deuteronomy, Israel is constantly reminded of its own past and present marginality as the basis for its care for the others who are also marginal—the widow, the poor, the orphan, and the sojourner.

Marginality also helps us to understand why those in the center have so much difficulty being truly evangelistic. This comes across quite clearly in the story of Paul and Barnabas in Antioch of Pisidia (Acts 13:13-52)—a story that is most important since it sets the pattern for much of the Pauline mission. Paul and Barnabas arrive at Antioch and attend the synagogue, where they are invited to speak. Paul gives a speech in which he reviews much of the history of Israel, ending with the startling announcement that the Promised One has come. Apparently, this was a very receptive synagogue, and one in which there were a number of Gentile "God-fearers"—people who, while accepting the moral and doctrinal teachings of Judaism, were not quite ready to embrace the entire law and become converts to Judaism. Note, for instance, that Paul repeatedly acknowledges this mixed audience: "You Israelites, and others who fear God" (13:16); "you descendants of Abraham's family, and others who fear God" (13:26). Thus, in spite of what we might expect, the people in the synagogue received Paul's message quite well, and "urged them to speak about these things again the next sabbath" (13:42). During the week, however, word got around the city, so that by the next sabbath "almost the whole city gathered to hear the word of the Lord" (13:44). It is at that point that Acts 13:45 tells us that "when the Jews saw the crowds, they were filled with jealousy," and turned against Paul and Barnabas. Apparently, these good, "liberal" Jews were quite willing to accept a few Gentiles in their midst. After all, the promise was that in the seed of Abraham all the nations would be blessed. But when there seemed to be a mass movement toward the synagogue to hear these preachers who spoke of the fulfillment of the hope of Israel, these very "liberal" Jews became jealous, and turned against the very preachers whom they had so readily accepted a week before.

Here we have a passage that has often been interpreted—along with many others—as justification for the anti-Semitic tendencies in the church. The Jews rejected the message because they were Jews.

But as we read the story from the perspective of marginality we recognize here one more instance of the manner in which good, enlightened, liberal people at the center often relate to those at the margins. The marginalized are welcome, so long as there are not too many of them and they do not threaten the privileges of the center. It was quite acceptable and even praiseworthy to welcome a few "God-fearers" to the synagogue; but when practically the entire city appeared at the door, that was just a bit too much. What would become of the synagogue? What of the privileges of the chosen people of God? After all, if too many are chosen then no one is chosen.

There are many other instances in the biblical narrative that deal with similar themes. Remember the prophet Jonah, who refused to go to Nineveh. I have lost count of the number of sermons I have heard about how Jonah feared to go to this distant land of cruel and evil people. But that is not what the story says. (Actually, when the storm hits at sea, the story depicts Jonah as a rather brave man who takes the blame and offers to be pitched overboard.) What Jonah actually says is that he did not want to go to Nineveh because he knew that God was a loving God who would forgive the hated Ninevites: "That is why I fled to Tarshish at the beginning; for I knew that you are a gracious God and merciful, slow to anger, and abounding in steadfast love, and ready to relent from punishing" (Jon. 4:2). In other words, he would have been quite willing to go had he expected God to really punish the hated Nineveh. But he knew God's mercy, and in this particular case he did not like it! Jonah's problem was that his theology told him that "the LORD, the God of heaven, who made the sea and the dry land" (1:9) is a God of mercy; and his nationalistic religion could not cope with it. Nineveh, powerful though it was—and precisely because it was a powerful and hated enemy—must remain marginal, distant from God's grace and forgiveness.

In Jonah we have an example of a relatively uncommon phenomenon in the Scripture: a successful prophet and a successful prophet who would rather have failed. The historical Jonah, son of Amittai, was a rather nationalistic prophet, supporting the territorial expansion of his nation (see 2 Kings 14:23-27). Can you imagine that Jonah returning to Israel and attempting to explain to Jeroboam and his generals that he had just been about the business of saving Nineveh from destruction?

It was for preaching the sort of message Jonah disliked that Jesus got in trouble in Nazareth. We often think that what the people there did not like was that Jesus claimed that the prophecy in Isaiah referred to him, saying "Today this scripture has been fulfilled in your hearing" (Luke 4:21). But look again at the text, and you will see that even after he said this "all spoke well of him and were amazed at the gracious words that came from his mouth" (4:22). So far, so good. One can even imagine the incipient pride in the townsfolk at the local boy who had become something: "Is not this Joseph's son?"

But Jesus suddenly changed his tune—or at least, it would seem so from the point of view of his audience. Until then he had said that they were at the very center of things. The Scripture was being fulfilled right there, "in your hearing." Now he tells them to expect no special privileges. He is not about to do in his hometown the things that he did at Capernaum. Furthermore, he tells them, remember the case of Elijah when there was a great famine in the land. He could have performed his miracles for the benefit of any of the many widows living in Israel at the time; but instead he went to a widow in Zarephath in Sidon—in other words, to a Gentile, unclean, marginal woman. And also Elisha could have healed any of the many lepers living in Israel at his time, yet the one who was cleansed was Naaman, a general from enemy Syria.

As we read this story taking into account what we know about the manner in which the center reacts when challenged by the margin we can easily understand why "when they heard this, all in the synagogue were filled with rage" (4:28). This was no longer a message about how they were at the very center of things, seeing the Scripture fulfilled before their eyes. This was rather a warning that they should expect no privileges, for God often works at the margins rather than the center. No wonder they tried to hurl him off a cliff!

Throughout his ministry, Jesus continued teaching and preaching along the same vein. Those who thought they belonged in the center, he put at the edges; and those who were usually condemned to look in from the sidelines, he placed at the center of his ministry and his promises. When the Pharisees complained to his disciples that he was eating and drinking with tax collectors and sinners,[1] he answered: "Those who are well have no need of a physician, but those who are sick" (Luke 5:31), which means that, unless you are ready to acknowledge that you are sick, Jesus is not for you! "He also told this parable to some who trusted in themselves that they were righteous and regarded others with contempt: 'Two men went up to the temple to pray, one a Pharisee and the other a tax collector. . . . I tell you, this man [the tax collector] went down to his home justified rather than the other; for all who exalt themselves will be humbled, but all who humble themselves will be exalted'" (Luke 18:9-14). And to others of similar attitude he said: "Truly I tell you, the tax collectors and the prostitutes are going into the kingdom of God ahead of you" (Matt. 21:31).

There are three parables in Luke 15 that we often misinterpret because we think they are addressed to the lost, rather than at the supposedly never lost. These are the parables of the lost sheep (Luke 15:3-7), the parable of the lost coin (Luke 15:8-10), and the parable of the prodigal son (Luke 15:11-32). These are excellent parables for evangelistic preaching, and therefore we have grown accustomed to telling them to those who in our estimation are lost, inviting them to be found or to come back to the loving Father. In this interpretation, if the parables refer at all to us religious people, they speak of the time when we were lost, and of God's great love and mercy for us. There certainly is value in that. It is important to tell those who are lost that God is looking for them. It is also important for us to rejoice in the mercy of God that has found us.

But there is another angle to all of these parables. According to Luke, they were not originally spoken to evil, sinful, unclean people. Luke tells us that the Pharisees and the scribes—that is, the best religious people of the time, and those who best knew the Scripture—were grumbling because Jesus was welcoming sinners and eating with them. It is at this juncture that "Jesus told *them* [the Pharisees and scribes] this parable." The three parables are not originally addressed to the lost, but to those who feel left out because Jesus is eating with the lost; to those who have never been lost. He is not speaking to the one lost sheep, but to the ninety-nine that the shepherd leaves "in the wilderness" in order to go look for the one. He is not speaking to the lost coin that the woman searches for until she finds it, but to the other nine that remain safely in her purse. He is not speaking to the prodigal son who has gone to a distant country, but to the elder son who has been serving his father all these years, resenting that he is working like a slave and yet he doesn't even get a young goat to celebrate a dinner with his friends. In short, Jesus is not speaking to the margin, but to the center. He is not merely speaking of God's love for the margin, but he is speaking of those who think they belong at the center, telling them that unless they too go out and seek the lost sheep and the lost coin, and welcome the younger brother, they are not true servants of this God. The God who, like a shepherd, seeks the lost one while even risking the ninety-nine; who, like a woman, seeks eagerly for a lost coin until she finds it; who, like a loving father, waits for the lost with open arms and a forgiving and celebrating heart.

This vision of the value of marginality is crucial, not only for reading the Scripture, but also for reading the history of the church, and even for reading our task as a church today. Throughout the history of the church, some of the most exciting things have happened, not at the traditional centers of the life of the church, but at the edges. Since in this chapter I have repeatedly mentioned Acts, look again at that book. As we begin reading the story, we expect the church in Jerusalem to be the most important church of all, the one that has all the answers and tells all the others what they ought to believe and do. Actually, most of us read through the entire book of Acts with that expectation still in mind, and therefore we fail to see much of what is really happening in that story.

But that is not the story as Acts tells it. The very first great event of Acts, Pentecost, the event that many call the birth of the church, is precisely an event of openness to outsiders. At the beginning of the story, the followers of Jesus are all gathered in a room, meeting among themselves. At the end of the story—and Luke does not tell us how they got from one place to another—they are outdoors, addressing a great crowd, and that crowd includes all sorts of people.

By the sixth chapter, as we have seen, we are dealing with the consequences of the addition of these new people to the community of faith. We are dealing with the problems caused by that addition, but also with the structural changes required by it. And very soon, as soon as Stephen starts preaching, we are dealing also with the increasing impact of Christianity on those around it. The result is persecution, dispersion, martyrdom—and growth!

But the growth is not only in numbers. If the story appears in Acts in chronological order, Philip, one of the seven, leads the way in preaching in Samaria, and also in the conversion of the Ethiopian eunuch. This happens in chapter 8. In chapter 9 we have not only the conversion of Saul, but also of Ananias. Ananias was already a disciple. But it is in the challenge of going to Saul, whom he knows as a terrible scourge of the church, that Ananias hears of the Lord's great plan, "to bring my name before Gentiles and kings and before the people of Israel" (9:15).

In chapter 10 we have what we usually call the conversion of Cornelius. It is the story of two visions and an encounter: the vision of Cornelius at Caesarea, the vision of Peter at Joppa, and the resulting meeting between Peter and Cornelius.

Let us begin by comparing the two visions.

First consider the vision of Cornelius at Caesarea. Cornelius is not a Jew. He is one of those Gentiles whom the Jews called "God-fearers," who hovered around Judaism, accepting many of its teachings. Although sympathetic to the faith of Israel, these God-fearers did not have the commitment to take the final step and join the people of God. Apparently most God-fearers were attracted by Jewish monotheism and by its moral teachings, but repelled by Jewish ceremonial practices, particularly circumcision.

This particular God-fearer, Cornelius, is a Roman citizen, for only men holding such citizenship could attain the rank of centurion, even in the auxiliary troops composed of noncitizens.

In contrast, the other vision comes to Peter, one of the Twelve, a faithful Jew who has followed Jesus for years. In his Gospel, Luke repeatedly portrays him as the spokesperson for the entire group of disciples. Likewise, the book of Acts also singles him out as the principal spokesperson for the followers of Jesus at Pentecost, and even before that, in the election of Matthias. In chapters 3 to 5 we have also been told that, together with John, he defied the Council that ordered them to be silent, and for that reason he had been persecuted and punished. If anyone was an insider in the new community of faith, that was Peter.

The story tells us that each of these two men had a vision. In the matter of such visions, we would expect Peter to take the lead. After all, he had taken the lead in confessing Jesus as the Christ, he had taken the lead at Pentecost, he had taken the lead in healing the lame man at the gate of the Temple, he had taken the lead in speaking before the Council, and he had taken the lead in spreading the word of Jesus throughout Judea.

But that is not what happens. Actually, the vision comes to Cornelius almost twenty-four hours before it comes to Peter. And before Peter even has his vision, the messengers that Cornelius has sent are already well on their way to the house where Peter is staying.

Furthermore, the text says quite explicitly that Cornelius's vision was clear: "he clearly saw an angel of God coming in" (10:3). And the angel told him exactly what he was to do, including the precise address where Peter could be found: ". . . send men to Joppa for a certain Simon who is called Peter; he is lodging with Simon, a tanner, whose house is by the seaside" (10:5, 6, 7). (Just about the only thing lacking was the zip code!)

In contrast, Peter's vision occurs when he is hungry and falls into a trance. And the vision is not altogether clear. We are told that he saw "*something* like a large sheet coming down" (11: 5). And there is a dialogue in which Peter stubbornly resists the voice that comes to him: " 'Get up, Peter; kill and eat.' But I replied, 'By no means Lord; for nothing profane or unclean has ever entered my mouth.' . . . 'What God has made clean, you must not call profane' " (11:7, 8, 9).

According to the text, this happened three times, and still Peter would not budge. Then, when "the thing" (that is what the text calls it) is finally taken up to heaven, we are told that "Peter was greatly puzzled about what to make of the vision that he had seen" (Acts 10:17).

Why is it that the vision of Cornelius is so much clearer than the vision of Peter? Perhaps we have a clue in the city where the vision of Peter takes place. That city is Joppa, well known in biblical literature for the acts of another messenger sent by God to a foreign people—a messenger whom we have already encountered in the present chapter. It was in Joppa that Jonah of old took ship for Tarshish in order to avoid the call of God to go to Nineveh. In that ancient story, we are told that the reason why Jonah refused to go to Nineveh was that he knew that Yahweh is a God of mercy and would forgive Nineveh. Jonah would have no part of it.

And now, again in Joppa, this other messenger, whose real name is Simon, *son of Jonah*, receives a similar call. God does not intend for him to go to faraway Nineveh. But Caesarea is far enough for any self-respecting, religious Jew.

Caesarea was not highly regarded by the more traditional Jews, for it was built by Herod the Great following the Roman pattern, and named in honor of Augustus Caesar. In it, as in any Hellenistic city, some of the main buildings were temples to the gods. Although there were Jews in Caesarea, other Jews often considered them inferior in their religious commitment, for they lived in a city where pagan practices were common, and where they could not avoid becoming ritually impure.

Caesarea is the symbol of Roman power and pagan uncleanness. We can only conjecture what Peter would have said if God had told him to go to Caesarea and baptize a group of heathen Romans. But, by the manner he reacted to the voice that said "kill and eat," it seems safe to surmise that he would not have been altogether pleased at the prospect. So, rather than a distinct command to go to Caesarea and bring Cornelius into the community of faith, Peter receives a vision whose meaning is not clear.

That meaning does not become clear at once. Rather, it is elucidated progressively, as Peter takes first one step and then another in obedience to the guidance of the Spirit. At first, the Spirit seems to call him away from his meditation on the meaning of the vision, simply telling him that some people are looking for him, and that he should go with them. Then he hears the messengers tell of Cornelius's vision. Still there is no word to him on the connection between the two visions; but, because the Spirit has told him to do so, Peter receives the messengers, and the next day he and a number of believers leave for Caesarea with the messengers.

Peter's first encounter with Cornelius and his friends is not felicitous by most modern missiological standards. First, when Cornelius falls at his feet and worships him, a common enough greeting for a Roman receiving an honored guest, Peter rejects that gesture rather rudely: "Stand up; I am only a mortal" (10:26). And then, when he finally enters the house where Cornelius has gathered his friends and kin, Peter's speech is not calculated to win friends and influence people: "You yourselves know that it is unlawful for a Jew to associate with or to visit a Gentile; but God has shown me that I should not call anyone profane or unclean" (10:28). In other words, if it were up to me, I would not associate with the likes of you. But God has told me that I must not call you unclean, even though that is precisely what I really would like to call you.

There is progress here. At least, Peter has begun to see the connection between his perplexing vision at Joppa and the call from Cornelius. But he still is not convinced. According to v. 22, Cornelius's messengers have already told him why he was sent for. But, in spite of that, Peter asks again: ". . . why you sent for me."

In spite of Peter's rudeness and limited vision, Cornelius insists, and tells him once again of the vision that Peter has already heard from the messengers sent to him. Eventually, Peter seems to get it, and says, "I truly understand that God shows no partiality, but in every nation anyone who fears him and does what is right is acceptable to him" (10:34). Now he is intellectually ready to share his message with these latter-day Ninevites, on whom God has decided to show mercy. So, he starts preaching a sermon, only to be surprised once again by the outpouring of the Spirit on his audience, to the point that finally he brings his newfound intellectual conviction into action: "Can anyone withhold the water for baptizing these people who have received the Holy Spirit just as we have?" (10:47).

This entire story is usually called the conversion of Cornelius. But when one reads it carefully, it is the conversion of Peter just as much as of Cornelius. Cornelius is converted from a God-fearer to a follower of the Way. Peter is converted from a follower of an exclusivistic Way, limited to those of his own heritage and traditions, to a proclaimer of a Way that is open to all persons, including the unclean Romans. In the encounter between Peter and Cornelius, it is not only Cornelius, but also Peter, who hears the gospel anew and is called to new obedience.

We usually read this passage in triumphalistic terms: one more step in the ever-widening circle of Christian outreach. What we miss is what the passage says about the Jewish Christians who had come with Peter. When they saw what was happening, they "were astounded that the gift of the Holy Spirit had been poured out even on the Gentiles" (10:45). Peter, who had felt rather uneasy about entering this house, now feels compelled to ask, "Can anyone withhold the water for baptizing these people who have received the Holy Spirit just as we have?' So he ordered them to be baptized." The radically new thing that is taking place here is not so much that a few more people are being baptized. It is not even that, apart from the Ethiopian eunuch, these may be the first Gentiles to be converted. It is rather that the church itself learns something about the gospel that it had not really understood before: that the gospel is Good News for *all* people.

The point is made quite clear in chapter 11, where Peter returns to Jerusalem to hear criticism from the church there: "Why did you go to uncircumcised men and eat with them?" (11:3). Peter tells them the story of what happened, and as a result, Luke tells us, "They praised God, saying, 'Then God has given even to the Gentiles the repentance that leads to life'" (11:18).

In other words, that what we have in these two crucial chapters of Acts is the conversion, not only of the Gentiles, but also and especially of Peter, of his Jewish Christian companions who went with him to Cornelius, and eventually of the entire church.

Perhaps our mistake has been that we have read the book of Acts, and much of later Christian history, as the history of the expansion of Christianity, when we should have read it also and primarily as the history of the conversion of Christianity.

The story of the church's conversion continues throughout the book of Acts. Paul does not fully conceive his mission to the Gentiles the moment he is converted. On the contrary, he discovers his mission in the very act of fulfilling it.

The Reverend Loida Martell-Otero, a Baptist minister in the Bronx, tells us that a case in point is the story of Lydia of Thyatira. According to Dr. Martell-Otero, "(Lydia) dares Paul to not only talk the talk but to walk the walk. To this apostle who has declared that 'in Christ Jesus there is no longer male nor female.' (Lydia) dares him, 'If you have judged me to be faithful to the Lord, come and stay at my home.' Paul is now being challenged." Significantly, as one looks at the context of this story, Dr. Martell-Otero's point becomes even stronger. Paul was in Philippi because in a vision "a *man* from Macedonia" had pleaded, "Come over to Macedonia and help us." The Greek leaves no doubt: the vision is of a male figure. In Philippi, on the sabbath, Paul and his companions go to a site outside the gate by the river, where they "supposed there was a place of prayer"—in other words, a synagogue. Instead of a synagogue, which required a minimum number of men present, what they find is a group of women. They sit down and speak to them. The result is the conversion and baptism of Lydia, who then "prevails" of Paul and his companions to accept her hospitality. One wonders whether the irony may not be intentional: Paul goes to Philippi on the basis of a vision of a *man*; he goes to a place where he expects to find a group of *men* leading worship; instead, he finds a *woman* who will become the mainstay of his work in Philippi! Thus, as Dr. Martell-Otero says, "The church is being made to convert, even as it seeks converts."

We all know that had it not been for the mission to the Gentiles, we would not be Christian. But, have we stopped to reflect on how much the church learned through that mission? Very little of our New Testament, if any, was written in Jerusalem. On the contrary, most of the New Testament was written precisely at that border between belief and unbelief, which has always been the growing edge of the Christian church, not only numerically, but also theologically.

True, the old center always thinks that it knows best, and the periphery even bows before it. Also true, sometimes the center has an important role to play by correcting something that is taking place at the growing edge. Thus, the church in Jerusalem sends Peter and John to Samaria to check up on what Philip has been doing, and they do have something of value to add to Philip's ministry. But quite often it is the periphery that drives the center to new discoveries.

In Acts 15 we learn that certain individuals from Judea, that is, from the center, took it upon themselves to make certain that all new converts would adjust to the theology and the practices of the center. So, Paul, Barnabas, and some others went to Jerusalem to settle the matter. The result was what is often called the Council of Jerusalem, which set the policies to be followed in the Gentile mission.

When considering that Council, however, three points are important. The first is that in that meeting in Jerusalem the Jerusalem Christians learned more than did those who represented the mission to the Gentiles. The second is that, although the policies for the Gentile mission were supposedly set in that Council, it is clear from the letters of Paul that the mission soon exceeded the bounds of such policies—see for instance the question of meat sacrificed to idols and the way Paul deals with it in 1 Corinthians 10. The third point is that, even though the church in Jerusalem apparently did not know it at the time, it would soon be Christians resulting from the Gentile mission who would become the financial mainstay for the entire Christian community, including that in Jerusalem—again, witness Paul's letters, and his insistence on the collection for Jerusalem.

What happened in New Testament times has happened throughout the history of the church. In the thirteenth century, when Western Christendom seemed to be at its best, with the Papacy at the height of its power under Innocent III, the most abiding ecclesiastical reforms did not come from that all-powerful pope. They came rather from the relatively small town of Assisi, where the son of a merchant, a young man so out of touch with the realities of Italian power and politics that his friends called him "Frenchy"—Francesco—took off the rich garments that his father had given him, dressed in a beggar's cloak and went to live and to preach among the poor. And now, centuries after the events, we know that of all the great things that Innocent III did—calling for a crusade, reorganizing much of the life and worship of the church, calling kings to task for their moral deviations—none was as significant for the life of the church as recognizing and acknowledging the power in the beggar from Assisi.

During that same thirteenth century, there were great universities in western Europe. Most famous among them was the University of Paris. Here was the center of Christian learning. Here were people trained with the greatest academic rigor of their time. If anyone in Western Christendom knew Christian tradition and theology, it was the theologians at the University of Paris.

Meanwhile, at the very edges of Western Christendom, in Sicily and in Spain, at the border between Christianity and Islam, a new challenge had been arising. Christian scholars had come into contact with the writings of Islam, as well as with Arabic translations of Aristotle and other ancient Greek philosophers. Translated into Latin, those writings made their way to the University of Paris. There some rejected them outright: Why should we worry about what those infidels have to say? We have the great Christian tradition. We are the University of Paris. Others accepted them uncritically, and soon found themselves beyond the bounds of Christian orthodoxy. But a third group, the most creative, took up the challenge, saw it as an opportunity, and developed a theology that eventually opened the way for the modern world.

The pattern appears over and over again: Luther with his theses, discovering that he had unleashed theological energies that he never suspected, even from the border town of Wittenberg, with its upstart university; Wesley reluctantly preaching to the miners in Bristol, and discovering dimensions of the gospel he had not suspected.

This may be precisely the reason why so-called "mainline" churches have so much difficulty with mission among Hispanics and other minorities. My own United Methodist Church has an outstanding record in mission in Korea, in Zaire, and in the Philippines. But our record is not so good among minorities in our own backyard.

The reason usually given in the case of Hispanics is that, after all, Hispanics are already Roman Catholics. Our "mainline" churches take an ecumenical stance, and it would be antiecumenical to engage in sheep-stealing. It is interesting to me that some of the very people who say that a missionary initiative directed at Latinos would be sheep-stealing are themselves trying to increase the membership of their own congregations by enticing members of other congregations in the same denomination! As we know, that is how most of the flourishing suburban congregations came to be.

What, then, is the real reason why in our so-called "mainline" Protestant denominations one so often hears that there is no need for mission among Latinos, and when there is such a mission it is often undertaken halfheartedly, as if in fear of success? The real reason is not that we want to avoid any semblance of sheep-stealing. The real reason is not that most Hispanics are Roman Catholic. The real reason is that the so-called "mainline" denominations are in fact "old-line," that they do not want to change, that they wish to remain at the center, to continue being "mainline," and that a certain intuition tells them that, were they to undertake significant mission among Hispanics, and be successful at it, our own mainline (or rather oldline) denominations would have to change.

We might call this the "Jonah syndrome." Jonah knew the mercy of God, and presumably rejoiced in it; but when that mercy was for others, he resented and resisted it. Likewise, there are many in our old-line denominations who are constantly calling for more evangelistic effort, but who balk at the changes this would bring about in the church. They want the church to grow in numbers, but not to change in composition. They want to evangelize, but they seem to think that the gospel is only for people like them—of their own race, class, culture, and educational level.

That is why our old-line denominations are so successful in mission, as long as there is salt water in between. Our promotional materials boast of the churches that are growing overseas among people of other cultures and races. But when mission involves bringing different people into *our* fold, right here at home, things are different. Salt water acts as a buffer, so that the center can be insulated from whatever is happening at the periphery, and not be *really* challenged by it. But when the periphery is close to home, when it is people who live in our own midst, we are afraid that they may tell us that there is a different way of being United Methodist, or Lutheran, or Presbyterian. A certain instinct tells us that radical evangelism in our society would bring about the conversion, not only of unbelievers, but also of the church. And that would be too threatening. Therefore we make certain that mission flows only in one direction: that the center can affect the periphery, but not vice versa. We translate materials into Spanish. We give money to support a Hispanic mission. We appoint a Hispanic pastor to go out there and work among Hispanics. But we are not ready to adjust our structures so that congregations made up mostly of poor people can be really viable. We are not ready to share our leadership, to open our cultural paradigms to the give-and-take that true encounter brings about. And then we wonder why our translations are not read, why our money brings so little result, and why our Hispanic pastor becomes frustrated and decides to go elsewhere. And so the Hispanic community—or any other minority community—is left without the resources that our faith and our churches could offer.

The loss is not only in the minority community. Our so-called "mainline" churches also suffer a serious loss. People wonder what is happening to the mainline churches, why our membership is declining, why our vitality is not what it used to be. There are many explanations, each with a certain degree of truth. But ultimately the reason why we are declining is that we have lost our sense of mission, and in so doing have lost one of the great sources from which the church has traditionally been renewed.

A reading from a perspective and experience of marginality tells the church that bringing the marginalized to the very center of God's love and God's community is an essential part of the gospel of Jesus Christ—so essential, that the doubt arises: In a society and a world in which so many are marginalized, is it legitimate for a church to call itself at the same time both "mainline" and "Christian"?

CHAPTER TWO

Poverty

lthough poverty is a particular instance or mode of marginality, it is sufficiently important as part of the Hispanic experience to deserve a separate chapter. This is not the place to repeat all the statistics regarding the poverty in which most Latinos live. Suffice it to say that, for over twenty years, every negative statistic for Hispanics—unemployment, underemployment, poverty rate, school dropouts—has remained at a steady 150 percent of what it has been for the rest of the population. (That is to say, for instance, that when unemployment stands at 8 percent for the rest of the population, it is 12 percent for the Latino population.) Whatever the statistics may be, the point is clear: in general, the Latino experience in the United States is one of poverty. (Which is not to say that such conditions are necessarily worse than in our various countries of origin. It is simply to say that the experience here and now most often includes poverty and lack of economic opportunity.) This means that, although most of us who write on Hispanic hermeneutics are not ourselves poor, we can only write about such a hermeneutics to the degree that we stand in solidarity with the vast majority of our people, who are indeed poor.

Thirty years ago, if confronted with the theme, "the Bible and the poor," I would have understood that to mean simply, what does the

Bible say about the poor? In order to answer that question, I would have thought that it would suffice for me to read the Bible, perhaps with the help of a concordance and a few scholarly books on the subject.

Today the situation is quite different. As I discussed in the Introduction, what has happened in the last decades is that we have become acutely aware that what one finds on the Bible depends to a large degree on one's perspective from which one reads the Bible. Thus, the question becomes more complicated. It is no longer simply, what does the Bible say about the poor? It is also and foremost, what does the Bible say when read from the perspective of the poor? Or, in other words, what do the poor find in the Bible that the nonpoor easily miss? Today, when we speak of "the Bible and the poor," the question is no longer simply, what can we discover in the Bible about the proper attitude of the church to the poor? The question is rather, what do the poor find in the Bible that is an important message to the entire church?

When looking at the Scripture from a perspective of poverty, or at least of solidarity with the poor, we find in it elements that we would not otherwise suspect. An interesting example of this was provided by Daniel García, who preaching on Genesis 22:1-14 (the sacrifice of Isaac) felt compelled, at least for a moment, to stand on the side of the ram that was sacrificed instead of Isaac. His point is that the powerful always find a convenient ram to be sacrificed at little or no cost to themselves:

> The poor and the impoverished of the land are sacrificed. Those who are caught in life's situations and circumstances are sacrificed. They are, so to speak, the convenient rams for the sacrifice, in order to spare the children of power. We know that those who exploit others always find someone for the sacrifice. That way, they avoid sacrificing themselves. They always find a convenient ram. But let us also remember that part of the teaching of this text about the intended sacrifice of Isaac is that human beings ought not to be sacrificed. The ram is an animal, and may be sacrificed. But when our farm-worker brothers and sisters are sacrificed, and so are so many others workers, sacrificed on the altar of capitalism, that is not right. That is sinful idolatry.[1]

Note that what García does here is to go beyond the mere antiquarian interpretation, which says simply that the purpose of this passage was to show that Israel's worship should not include human sacrifice. He also moves beyond the more existentialist interpretation, à la Kierkegaard, which turns the passage into a dreadful encounter with the awesome God who might require the sacrifice of Isaac. While retaining the basic thrust of the passage against human sacrifices, García reads it, so to speak, "from the margin," or from the perspective of the ram, and thus realizes that the passage is still quite relevant, for there are many people, even today, who are "convenient rams" for the sacrifice of the powerful.

Another case in which the experience of poverty led a preacher to interpret a passage in a rather unusual way took place in a very impoverished urban community. The pastor had been preaching on the Ten Commandments, and came to the law regarding the sabbath: "Six days you shall labor and do all your work. But the seventh day is a sabbath to the LORD your God" (Deut. 5:13). The most common interpretation of this passage is rather legalistic, as if for some capricious design God had decided that one day in seven would be for rest, and now it were our task to spell out that law in its minutest detail. That was the sort of interpretation against which Jesus had to struggle constantly, and which has repeatedly appeared in the Christian church. Another rather common interpretation turns the commandment regarding the sabbath into a religious law, stipulating that this is a day set aside for worship, as if God required one day in seven. Clearly, the text says nothing about this, for the worship of God on this particular day is not even mentioned. And in any case it would be rather uncharacteristic for the sovereign God of all creation to demand one day in seven—as if the rest were not also holy! A more enlightened interpretation realizes the joy and the celebration intended in the sabbath law. The sabbath is the day in which we rest, just as God rested; in which we rejoice in our work, just as God saw that creation was good; in which not only we, but also the animals and even the earth, join in the blessed and joyful rest of God.

But in this particular church the preacher followed none of these avenues. Rather, he began by asking how many in the congregation had been able to work six days during the previous week. A few hands went up. He then asked how many had been able to work five days. A few more hands. Four Days? More hands. Then he asked, "How many of you were not able to find work at all?" More than half of the congregation raised their hands. Finally, he asked, "How many of you wish you could work six days a week, but can't find work?" Almost every hand went up.

At that point, the preacher read the text again: "Six days you shall labor and do all your work." He stopped, and asked, "How, then, are we to obey the law of God, that commands that we shall work six days, when we cannot even find work for a single day?"

Perhaps this particular preacher was more inflammatory than necessary. But the point is that, as one profoundly identified with a population where unemployment, and not overemployment, is the great evil, he saw in the commandment something most of us do not see. The commandment says that we must rest, yes; but it says that in the context of work. It says that in a context in which it is expected that all will have employment. The order that the commandment envisions is one in which people will take the time to rest, and give the same time to other people as well as to animals and the whole of creation. But that rest is envisioned within a context of work. "Six days you shall work" is no less part of the order that God envisions and desires than resting on the seventh day. The commandment is not only to rest. It is also a commandment to work.

Clearly, in an agrarian society in which most households had a plot of land, and in which there was always work to be done, the emphasis lay on the need to set aside a day for rest. In such a society, one could easily work seven days a week, with no respite, and expect similar work from animals, servants, and employees. Against such practices, the law rightly sets aside a day for rest. The point at which the law was most likely to be broken was in working more than the six days, and leaving no time for rest. Thus, it is not surprising that in much of the most ancient tradition of interpretation the emphasis lay on the day of rest.

It is true that we still need laws guaranteeing rest. Unfortunately in recent times, with our twenty-four hours a day, seven days a week competitive economy, the principles of rest are being increasingly violated. Christians are often incensed at the manner in which the laws regarding the day of rest are being eroded. And they should be; but not for the reasons often adduced. The problem is not that an increasingly secular society is impinging on God's day. The problem is that an increasingly inhumane society driven by the maximization of profits is impinging on the very order of creation, in which all—people, animals, and even the land—require rest as well as work. Significantly, as the old laws requiring that stores close on Sundays disappear, those who end up losing their rest are the poor, who must work at whatever times they are told, and whose services must be available to the rich twenty-four hours a day, seven days a week. The sabbath was not ordered for the sake of a God who requires worship. The sabbath was ordained for the sake of a creation that requires rest.

Yet what the preacher that I have quoted was driving at was much more radical than this. What he was driving at is that the reason why we have centered our attention on the day of rest to the exclusion of the days of work is that most biblical interpretation has been done by those who do not have to worry about work. These are mostly two categories of people: those who do not have to work at all, and those who normally have employment, but who need the guarantee that they will not be overworked by their employers. Historically, there has been much tension between these two groups, and it is in that context that the labor laws were forged determining the number of work hours in a regular week, and other such matters. In the tension between these two groups, which has existed since time immemorial, the commandment regarding rest has played an important role.

That debate, however, has left aside an ever-increasing number of people in our modern societies whose problem is not having a day off, but having work to do. Although society does not determine exactly who these people will be by giving them actual names, society does determine that there will be a certain level of unemployment, and that people at the bottom rungs of the economic ladder will have to fight among themselves for the relatively few number of jobs available to them. These were the people to whom this particular preacher was speaking. (Unfortunately, they are also the people who often know all of this without having to be told.) Still, the point is clear: the reason why we do not see that the commandment is also about the right to work is that most of us are not in that predicament. Christians who are so incensed about the erosion of the sabbath laws should be even more incensed at the fact that our society has never even considered the possibility that the right to work may be a God-given right—for God does not command us to do what we cannot do.

One of the points at which a consciousness of poverty illumines the text of Scripture is the parables of Jesus. Scholars have noted that the parables of Jesus speak mostly of two social classes, the rich landowner, and the poor peasant, servant, or day laborer.[2] Yet most interpretation of the parables is done from a middle-class perspective that has little understanding of either of those two classes, or of the struggles that the parables reflect.

Take for instance the parable of the laborers in the vineyard, in Matthew 20:1-16. The story clearly depicts two kinds of people: the landowner and the laborers that he hires. The story is simple: the landowner goes early in the morning to the place where laborers are waiting to be hired, and after agreeing that he will pay them a denarius—the usual daily wage—sends them to his vineyard. Then he goes back at later times (nine o'clock, noon, three o'clock, and five o'clock) and each time hires additional laborers, making with them a vague contract that they will be paid for their work. At the end of the day, the laborers are paid in the reverse order in which they were hired. The last, who were hired at five o'clock, receive a whole denarius. When the first, who did work a whole day, also receive a denarius, they grumble that the landowner is unfair. But the landowner responds that they have been paid a fair wage, and that he is free to do with what is his as he wishes. They have no right to complain about his generosity toward those who worked less, and still received a full day's wage.

When this story is read in most churches, there is a general reaction that the whole thing is unfair. It is just not right that people who worked more should be paid the same as people who worked less. In that social context, all that is seen is the injustice, and the sermon then usually argues that God's grace is above justice.

In contrast, when the parable is read in some of our poor Hispanic churches there are people who immediately identify with the laborers, for they understand the plight of those who must go early in the morning to stand at a place where someone may come in a pickup truck and hire them. They may be lucky one day and find a whole day's work. Other days, they may spend hours waiting, and find nothing to do, or be hired only for a couple of hours. They clearly understand, because they have experienced it, the conversation between the landowner and those who are still standing around at about five o'clock: "Why are you standing here idle all day?" "Because no one has hired us." Then comes the surprising finale, where the landowner pays those who only worked a couple of hours a whole day's wage, and the reaction is not one of mystification and outrage, as in a middle-class congregation, but rather of joy and celebration. They can see that this is not an act of injustice, but rather an act of supreme justice. Those hired at five o'clock were not at fault in not having found work earlier. They were actually standing there all day, hoping against hope that someone would hire them. In a sense, they had more hope and stamina than those who were guaranteed a job early in the day. The fact that no one hired them does not mean that they will not have to eat, or that their needs will be lesser. They too need a day's wages in order to survive. Thus, the landowner's act in paying them a full day's wage is not a show of a grace that goes against justice, but rather of a grace that understands justice at a deeper level than is customary. The landowner pays them what they justly need and what they justly deserve, not what society, with its twisted understanding of justice, would pay them. Common justice would wash its hands of any responsibility for these unfortunate ones who did not find enough work to earn a living. This utterly just landowner, in contrast, pays them what they need, and what they would have been ready to earn had they been hired earlier.

In a way, the common reaction of most congregations is similar to the reaction of those who were hired earlier. They worked a full day; they had earned their day's wage; they deserve more than the rest.

The less fortunate do not deserve a full day's wage. They may need it; but they have not earned it, and should not be paid for work they did not do. What we forget, and those laborers also forget, is that we have been able to work and make a living because, in a world that is still much as that described in the parable, we have been more fortunate than others. Thus, we are ready to limit "justice" to that which recompenses us and others like us for our full-time, hard work. If we are callous, we may even say that those who have no work should simply be left to fend for themselves. If we are more sensitive, we may argue that such people need help, either through private charity or through public welfare. We may even provide for them out of our own resources. And all of this is good. But still we shall most likely miss the point, that this parable is not speaking of God's grace as the opposite of justice, but rather as a higher and more loving understanding of justice.

A second parable that looks different when read from the perspective of the poor is the story of the unforgiving servant in Matthew 18:23-35. We usually read the parable and get the main point: the servant to whom much was forgiven was unwilling to forgive a much smaller debt, and therefore the king rescinded his act of forgiveness. But look at the figures involved, remembering the social status of most of Jesus' hearers, and the parable becomes much more poignant—and even contemporary. Ten thousand talents, the amount that the king's servant was forgiven, would have been the equivalent of 150,000 years of work for a laborer. Given the average wage for Hispanics in the United States, it would be for us the equivalent of one and a half billion dollars. These are the sort of sums that we hear bandied about in discussions on the national budget or the S & L scandal. They are figures so large that we have no conception of them. Then the lesser debt is for 100 denarii. This was a little over three months' wages. It was a common sum that would have touched Jesus' audience as something they could have experienced. In an agricultural society, with cyclical employment, it was not uncommon for someone to owe that much while waiting for the next harvest. It was also not uncommon for someone to lose land, freedom, and family over such a sum. This too is a figure with which most Hispanics can relate, for an overdue debt that is the equivalent of three months' wages is quite common in our impoverished communities—and may often lead to eviction.

What we overlook here is that Jesus was speaking of a common experience in his time, and also in ours. The very rich did not have to pay their debts, for they usually were also very powerful. The poor, on the other hand, often found that their debts were a burden from which they could not free themselves—to the point that it was common for poor debtors to sell themselves into slavery. Thus, in people's minds, a debt of 10,000 talents was very different from a debt of 100 denarii—just as in today's way of thinking, a debt or a deficit of $1.5 billion is very different from a debt of $3,000. The larger figure relates to people who live in the stratosphere of society, who handle government budgets and contracts, or who get rich with schemes such as the S & L scandal. It is not a debt that anyone expects will have to be paid, just as few expect the major figures in the S & L scandal to go to jail, or the presidents of corporations who overcharge the government for billions of dollars to be treated as criminals. But the smaller debt is another matter. That better be paid, or your wages will be garnished and you will be evicted from your overcrowded apartment.

The reaction of Jesus' hearers must have been similar to the reaction of a poor Latino community meeting in a storefront church where the rent is overdue. Jesus is speaking of a truly just king! Once again, true justice is not the opposite of mercy, but rather its companion. But this is mercy applied justly, so that if the S & L executive or the real estate agent insists that Delia's rent be paid on time, even though Delia is temporarily unemployed, or else she and her family will be evicted, the government will also insist that the executive pay his or her debts, or else go to jail!

Naturally, this was not the way the Roman government worked. The emperor's favorites did not pay their debts, and then became richer by extorting the poor out of their lands and liberty. Nor is this the way our systems of banking and of justice work. Thus, the parable could and can be heard, yes, as a call for constant and liberal forgiving, as we usually hear it; but it would and can also be heard as a critique of a social order which, while calling itself just, knows how to temper justice with mercy for the rich, but not for the poor.

A final example in which the consciousness of poverty has illumined a parable is in a Bible study by Jorge E. Sánchez on Luke 11:5-13. Commenting on that parable, Sánchez pointed out that what we have here is a typical experience among the poor. First of all, the man is already in bed with his family, and cannot get up without waking and disturbing all of them. This makes no sense in our modern, middle-class houses. This family, like so many poor families throughout the world, must sleep together, all in the same room and the same bed. Second, the man who comes to ask is also poor. We usually imagine that what the parable means is that this man cannot go and buy food for his unexpected visitor because it is late at night and the supermarket is closed. Knowing how poor families must live and make do, Sánchez points out that this is not the case. The man is simply poor, and a friend has arrived whom he cannot feed. Therefore, he goes and asks for help from another friend, who is also poor. There is nothing unusual about this. The man who asks is not particularly bold or daring. He is simply behaving according to the laws of hospitality, which the poor in ancient times understood much in the same way as the modern poor: the need of the unexpected arrival becomes the need of the unprepared host, who in turn calls on another, probably equally poor, to make it also her or his need.

When one reads it in this context, the point of the parable is no longer—as we often hear on radio and television—that God will give us anything we ask for, but rather that God, as a neighbor in solidarity with the poor, will help us meet the needs of love and hospitality, no matter how poor we are. The man in the parable asked from his friend for another friend; the man in the parable is needy out of solidarity with his visiting friend; and it is to that need that the friend whom he awakens responds.

It is within this context of solidarity and hospitality among the poor that one must understand the two often quoted and just as often misunderstood summaries in which the book of Acts describes the economic life of the early church:

All who believed were together and had all things in common; they would sell their possessions and goods and distribute the proceeds to all, as any had need. (Acts 2:44-45)

Now the whole group of those who believed were of one heart and soul, and no one claimed private ownership of any possessions, but everything they owned was held in common. With great power the apostles gave their testimony to the resurrection of the Lord Jesus, and great grace was upon them all. There was not a needy person among them, for as many as owned lands or houses sold them and brought the proceeds of what was sold. They laid it at the apostles' feet, and it was distributed to each as any had need. (Acts 4:32-35)

As we look at these texts, the first thing to be noted is that interpreters have often sought ways to diminish their importance.

One way of interpreting these texts to avoid their radical implications is to say that the early community did indeed practice a commonality of goods, but soon abandoned this practice. According to this commonly held notion, the failure of this practice soon convinced Christians that their original zeal was unjustified, and that having things in common was a mistake. As a result, it is claimed, the entire idea was forgotten a few years—perhaps months—after Pentecost.

A second way that the implications of this text are avoided is by taking the opposite direction and claiming that the commonality of goods described in Acts never happened. According to this interpretation, Luke is simply projecting back into the early days of the church an ideal that he actually took from Hellenism. There was a long tradition in Greek philosophy, dating back to Pythagoras and even earlier, and including Plato, which saw the common possession of goods as a characteristic of the ideal society. Therefore, so the argument goes, what Luke is actually doing here is simply projecting that ideal back onto the early Christian community.

The main difficulty with such an interpretation is that, as we read the book of Acts, it is unlikely that we will come to the conclusion that Luke is trying to picture an ideal community. This is the community of Ananias and Sapphira, and the community where the widows of the Hellenists find it necessary to complain that they are not getting a fair share.

In any case, both of these explanations go against the most common principles of historical scholarship. When looking at ancient historical texts, scholars usually expect that the practices and ideals of the time at which the document was written have been projected back to the time to which the document refers. In dealing, for instance, with the various gospel accounts of the life of Jesus, scholars are quick to point out those elements in such accounts that reflect conditions, not at the time of Jesus, but at the time of the actual writing of the gospel.

But when it comes to the texts in Acts that speak of an original commonality of goods among Christians, it is customary to take the opposite tack, declaring that such commonality was probably a fleeting experiment that failed, or something that never happened. Were we to apply to these texts the same principles applied elsewhere, we would come to the conclusion that, no matter whether or not the very early church practiced such commonality, at the time when the book of Acts was written this was either the practice or the ideal of the church.

In consequence, it seems logical to conclude that, at least at the time when the book of Acts was written, the church was practicing, or trying to practice, a commonality of goods such as the one described in our texts. That this was true, not only in Luke's time, but even much later, is clear from the historical evidence.

There is ample textual proof that, even after the time of Luke, Christians were speaking of the commonality of goods as something that was still practiced among them. In 1875, a long lost document was discovered in Istanbul. The date of this document, called the *Didache* or *Teaching of the Twelve Apostles,* is difficult to determine, but most scholars agree that it was written sometime between the year 60 and the first decades of the next century. In other words, it is roughly contemporary with the book of Acts. There we find words that remind us of the text we are studying:

You shall not turn the needy away, but rather will share everything with your brother [or sister], and call nothing your own. Since you already share in immortal goods, should you not do so even more in those that are mortal? (4:8)

Almost exactly the same words are found in the so-called *Epistle of Barnabas* (19:8), probably written around the year 130. Likewise, Tertullian, writing around the year 200, declares:

All of us who are joined in one heart and soul do not hesitate in sharing material goods. All things are common among us, except women.

Thus, the notion that the texts we are studying in Acts are pure Lukan fiction, or that they refer only to a fleeting moment in the life of the early church, is clearly shown to be wrong.

There is, however, another way in which this text has been interpreted so as to diminish its challenge to us. That is by overradicalizing it. According to this interpretation, what this text means is that, as a result of their overwhelming experience, the early Christians sold all they had—or as we would say today, used up their principal— and soon they were all left in poverty. There are even commentators who then tell us that this failed experiment was the reason why Paul had to spend so much of his time collecting an offering for the church in Jerusalem! Such is the view expressed, for instance, by G. H. C. Macgregor in *The Interpreter's Bible*:

Probably also the eager expectation of the Parousia led to improvidence for the future, so that the Jerusalem community was always poor. Accordingly we find the selling of local possessions superseded by the sending of alms to the mother church by the richer daughter churches.[3]

Likewise, another modern scholar declares that:

. . . the trouble in Jerusalem was that they turned their capital into income, and had no cushion for hard times, and the Gentile Christians had to come to their rescue.[4]

This is simply not what the text says. In Greek, there are two forms of the past tense. (I may add that the same is true in Spanish, that other vehicle of divine revelation!) One of these forms of the past tense, the imperfect, refers to an ongoing action in the past (as in "When I was in college I went to the movies on Saturdays"). The other refers to a single action in the past (as in "I went to the movies Saturday"). In both cases, the verb is "went"; but in the first case I mean that I used to go, while in the other I mean that I went once and for all.

In Acts, the past tenses are in the imperfect. Thus, what the text means is not that the early believers went out and sold everything, but rather that they would sell their possessions and goods, and would distribute them, "as any had need" (Acts 2:45).

This was not a modern commune, guided by some ideological dream of common property. It was simply a community of love, guided by the need of the less fortunate—an experience not so distant from the practice even this day in many poor communities both among Latinos in the United States and in Latin America. Actually, the notion of a commune as an ideological principle brought to practice is much more typical of the middle and high classes, where need is generally an abstraction, or is confused with desire. Among the poor, the sharing of goods is often a necessary means of survival, something that one practices, not out of an ideological commitment, but simply because without it the community could not survive.

Since I have just used the word *community,* it may be well to clarify another point, closely related to this subject, at which we have weakened the language of the New Testament. We all know, or think we know, that *koinonía* means "fellowship." What we are not usually told is that it means much more than what we today mean by "fellowship." In some ways, it comes closer to "partnership," as in a business venture. Thus in Luke 5:10, the NRSV tells us that James and John, the sons of Zebedee, were "partners" with Simon. What the Greek says is that they were *koinonoi* with him. In the common secular language of the time, if a group of us were to join in a common business venture, being common owners of it, what we would have would be a *koinonía.* Thus, *koinonía* does not mean simply "fellowship" or "communion." It also means partnership in the sense of sharing in material or any other kind of wealth. Therefore, when the New Testament speaks of the *"koinonía* of Jesus Christ," or of the *"koinonía* of the Spirit," it does not mean simply, as we often think, the good feeling of fellowship engendered in us by Jesus Christ or by the Spirit. It means also our common participation, in a way our common ownership, in Jesus Christ or in the Spirit. And it also means our partnership in all things because of Jesus Christ or because of the Spirit.

If on that basis we look at the entire New Testament, we find that this kind of sharing, not only in the spiritual sense, but also in the material, appears throughout. Whenever the church is spoken of as a *koinonía*, what is meant is, among other things, a company in which all are equal stockholders, so that all each has is at the disposal of the rest.

The clearest example of this is the collection for the church in Jerusalem, which plays a fairly prominent role in the letters of Paul. As was mentioned, some interpreters have claimed that the church in Jerusalem became poor because they had sold all they had, eaten the proceeds, and been left with nothing to live on. There is nothing in the New Testament to support such an interpretation. On the contrary, there is every indication, supported by both pagan and Jewish historians, that there was a general famine in Palestine at this time. If such was the case, what most likely happened was that the church in that region, composed mostly of people of meager means, was sorely tried to meet the most urgent needs of the poorest among them.

In Romans 15:25-27, Paul explains to the Romans that his hope for visiting them has to wait until he finishes his work on the offering for the Jerusalem church: "for Macedonia and Achaia have been pleased to establish a partnership [a *koinonía*] with the poor among the saints in Jerusalem." (Thus the RSV. The NRSV says, instead of "to establish a partnership," "to share their resources.") Paul then goes on to say that these Gentiles "were pleased to do this, and indeed they owe it to them; for if the Gentiles have come to share in their spiritual blessings, they ought also to be of service to them in material things."

Paul also needs to remind the Achaians—particularly the church in Corinth—to fulfill what they had promised to the suffering church in Jerusalem. In 2 Corinthians 8, he does so:

> It is appropriate for you who began last year not only to do something but even to desire to do something—now finish doing it. . . . I do not mean that there should be relief for others and pressure on you, but it is a question of a fair balance between your present abundance and their need, so that their abundance may be for your need, in order that there may be a fair balance. As it is written, [in Exodus 16], "The one who had much did not have too much, and the one who had little did not have too little."
>
> (2 Cor. 8:10-11, 13-15)

In this passage, as a theological prod, Paul reminds the Corinthians of what happened in the Exodus, as recorded in Exodus 16. We generally remember the miracle of the manna—that God gave the "bread from heaven" for the Israelites in the wilderness—but we often overlook the miracle that Paul reminds his Christians readers of in this passage: the miracle of the distribution. When the manna fell, the head of each "tent" went out to collect enough for the family, to be measured at about a quart apiece. Some gathered much more than they should have, and others did not get enough (a typical human situation!). However, when they came to measure it, a miracle occurred: those who had gathered too much found that the excess had disappeared, and those who had too little found their supply had increased to the right amount. God had performed a miracle to make the sharing in the resources provided come out right. (Perhaps one of the reasons we tend to remember the miracle of production, and not the miracle of distribution, is that as a culture and as a society we can boast of imitating God in being productive, but not in the manner our resources are distributed.)

In both Romans and Corinthians, Paul calls for a sharing both in material and in spiritual goods. The Gentiles had received and were still receiving a share in the spiritual resources of the Jerusalem church, and therefore ought to share with them the material resources that they possessed. It is the same expectation we saw in the

Didache: If we share in immortal goods, ought we not also share in mortal ones?

One could raise from these passages the question whether churches that are materially poor often have spiritual gifts to share with those churches that are richer materially. Although clearly this cannot be universally assumed, it is often the case.

There is an interesting passage in Proverbs that points to the dangers of too little material wealth as well as too much: both conditions pose spiritual dangers:

> Two things I ask of you;
>   do not deny them to me before I die:
> Remove far from me falsehood and lying;
>   give me neither poverty nor riches;
>   feed me with the food that I need,
>   or I shall be full, and deny you,
>   and say, "Who is the LORD?"
>   or I shall be poor, and steal,
>   and profane the name of my God.
> (Prov. 30:7-9)

The phrase "the food that I need" refers to the daily ration of a soldier—the proper share, neither too much nor too little. It is that phrase that lies behind the Exodus story. It also occurs in the Lord's Prayer: "Give us this day our daily bread." What is meant is the right portion for us, with a clear understanding that too much can be as dangerous as too little.

In the case of the collection for the Jerusalem church, Paul is pointing out that sharing the material resources can help both Jerusalem and Corinth. The collection would help balance things out so both churches had the right amount. What Paul has done is that he has gone beyond the local congregation. The *koinonía* is world-wide. Therefore, the sharing of resources seeking to prevent there being any needy among the community is also global.

Putting all of this together, it is clear that the community described in the book of Acts, in their readiness to share and to meet the

73

material needs of all of the members, is living out the meaning of the Lord's Prayer. No wonder there is not a needy person among them.

As for Luke/Acts, scholars have pointed out that the term "poor" in the sense of the absolutely destitute—*ptochos*—which is quite common in Luke, does not appear in Acts. Could it be that the author's mind has somehow changed between the two treatises? Or is it rather that what Acts is saying is that in the community of the Spirit the promise of Deuteronomy is fulfilled, that "there will, however, be no one in need among you . . . if only you will obey the LORD your God"? (Deut. 15:4-5). From all that the book of Acts says about the sharing of resources and its connection with the outpouring of the Spirit, the latter would seem to be the most adequate explanation.

Finally, it is important to recognize that, although for purposes of ease of exposition I have separated poverty from marginality as a paradigm for interpretation, in actual Latino experience these two, as well as the other paradigms, are all of one piece. For many of us, poverty has been the reason why we had to leave our lands of origin and travel to a land where we would still be generally poor—although perhaps not quite in the same way—and where we would be permanently marginalized aliens (an issue we shall discuss in chapter 4). For others whose roots in this land are deep and ancient, poverty has come together with marginalization and alienation from our own culture, traditions, and identity (an issue we shall discuss in chapter 3). This was seen and expressed in a sermon by Yolanda Pupo-Ortiz:

> The reality of the doctrine of Manifest Destiny reminded me of the incident of the vineyard of Naboth and King Ahab. . . . The vineyard was all Naboth had. But that was not the only reason for its importance. The vineyard was dear to Naboth's heart because it was an inheritance from his parents. An inherited land was never sold in Israel; yet the King disregarded all of that. To take away the vineyard was to take away Naboth's humanity: his connection to his parents, tradition, and beliefs.[5]

What Pupo-Ortiz is pointing out here is that poverty is much more than the lack of things. It certainly is that; but it is much more.

Poverty

Poverty, as experienced by vast numbers of Hispanics in our barrios and in our migrant camps, is dehumanization. It dispossesses, not only of money, but also of dignity, of tradition, of identity. At the same time and on the other hand, exile itself is a form of poverty. It does not rob one of money. Perhaps it even improves one's economic condition. But it is also a form of poverty inasmuch as it deprives one of identity, traditions, roots, dignity, family.

Mestizaje and Mulatez

One paradigm that is very significant for many of us is *mestizaje,* the experience of being *mestizos*—that is, mixedbreeds—and all that goes with it. One of the immediate results of the Spanish conquest of the Western Hemisphere was miscegenation between the Spanish and the Native peoples, whose offspring were called *mestizos.* Traditionally, this was a pejorative term, by which the Spaniards or the "pure" *criollos* who were their descendants justified their control of power and wealth, and the oppression of the Indian as well as of the *mestizo.* A similar process took place with the introduction of slaves from Africa, with the difference that the offspring of white and black parents was called a *mulatto*—another pejorative term.[1] These words were used pejoratively to such an extent, that *mestizos* themselves, as well as *mulattos,* often believed that their condition was by nature inferior.

It was the Mexican Revolution that began to change these attitudes by reaffirming the value of the indigenous in Mexican culture, and by promoting justice and equality for the Indian as well as the *mestizo* population. At a later date, the worldwide movement promoting pride in "negritude" played a similar role for the black and the mulatto. In 1925, as part of the intellectual upheavals connected with the Mexican Revolution, Mexican philosopher José Vasconcelos published an epoch-making book under the title *La raza cósmica: La misión de la raza iberoamericana* (*The Cosmic Race: The Mission of the Iberoamerican Race*). Although since surpassed by others who have expanded and corrected his views, Vasconcelos was the first major author since the times of the Conquest to propose a philosophical basis for pride in the mixture of races that has resulted in what he called "the cosmic race."[2]

More recently, Father Virgilio P. Elizondo, founder of the Mexican American Cultural Center in San Antonio and currently Rector of the Cathedral of San Fernando in San Antonio, has done most significant work with this understanding of our reality. He explored this subject both in his doctoral dissertation for the Institute Catholique in Paris and in his book *Galilean Journey: The Mexican-American Promise*, whose publication may be said to mark the beginning of Hispanic theology in the United States.[3] The Mexican, he says, is born out of the *mestizaje* of the Spanish and the Indian; the Mexican-American, out of the *mestizaje* of the Mexican and the Anglo. *Mestizaje* is a threat to both its parent cultures, for it undermines "the barriers of separation that consolidate self-identity and security."[4] It also points toward the future, for all culture and all ethnic identity is provisional, and eventually gives way to a new *mestizaje*.

All of these positive things, however, do not imply that *mestizaje* is an easy condition in which to live. Elizondo states the contrary quite forcefully:

> The cultural parent groups of the *mestizo* normally tend to reject their cultural child and its cultural identity because it does not appear to be the perfect mirror of their own identity. The *mestizo* is partly their own, but it is partly other and foreign. As a *mestizo* you are allowed to live, but you are not allowed to have a life of your own. You will always appear deficient by the norms of both parent groups and therefore never fully acceptable to either. Yet the parent cultures are not destroyed in the *mestizo,* but mutually combined so as to form a new identity. The great tragedy of *mestizo* existence is that the parent cultures do not see their child in a loving way, but rather tend to look

upon it as a mixture of "good and bad," a misfit, a nonequal. If cultural-spiritual poverty is the worst type of oppression, *mestizaje* is the worst type of human rejection because it brings with it a *double* alienation and margination.[5]

Although Elizondo is writing as a Mexican-American, other Latinos have similar experiences of *mestizaje*. Professor Robert W. Pazmiño, of Andover-Newton Theological School, reports:

I am an Hispanic-North American, a new breed Hispanic. My ethnic roots are Ecuadorian in my father's lineage and Dutch and German from Pennsylvania in my mother's lineage. . . . A person who is Hispanic-North American is conscious of being at a point represented by the position of the hyphen in that term, the position of navigating and balancing the convergence of two cultures which rotate in distinct orbits and require careful consideration and balance.[6]

Those elements of Hispanic population where the mixture has been mostly of European and African stock have similar experiences, although in this case understood as *mulatez*. Just as Mexican culture is *mestizo* culture, no matter whether one is of Spanish or of Indian descent, so is the culture of the Latin Caribbean predominantly *mulatto* culture, no matter who one's ancestors may have been. Or, perhaps more accurately, Latino culture is an admixture of all these elements, in varying proportions according to different regions and situations. In situations where *mulatez* is dominant, there are deeply ingrained internalizations of antiblack prejudice, even among the *mulatto* population—a prejudice that is therefore directed against oneself. Thus, it is not uncommon to hear a parent encouraging a child to marry someone of lighter skin or *pelo bueno*—good hair—in order to *mejorar la sangre*—to improve the blood. As in the case of *mestizaje,* however, there is an increasing sense of pride in some circles where a generation ago the predominant mood was one of self-deprecation.

One sees that recovery of pride in Pablo Jiménez, a Puerto Rican of mixed European and African heritage, when he comments on Philippians 2:7, "[Christ] emptied himself, taking the form of a slave": "The Prince of the Universe became a slave! This word has a chilling effect on me. My grandfather was a black man, the son of free slaves who toiled in the southern part of the island in Puerto Rico." And then (in another sermon) he goes on to speak of love as God's *carimbo*—the hot iron with which slaves were branded. If Christians are God's slaves, he says, love is our brand—and it is not an easy brand, but one which sears the flesh and even the heart.

For all Latinos in the United States, *mestizos* as well as *mulattos*, there is a further *mestizaje* or *mulatez*: our own relationship with the dominant culture. This is particularly true of those who are not first-generation immigrants. As Elizondo says, a Mexican-American is the result of a double *mestizaje*: first, of Indian and Spanish, to produce the Mexican; second, of Mexican and North American, to produce the Mexican-American. The same is true of the Puerto Rican in Chicago, the Dominican in New York, or the Cuban in Miami. There is always a sense of belonging and yet not belonging, of being both fish and fowl, and therefore fowl to the fish, and fish to the fowl; but also able to understand the fish as no fowl can, and the fowl as no fish can.

The implications of this paradigm for biblical interpretation are obvious. We read much of the Bible from a perspective of ethnic and cultural purity. But there are also other trends in the Bible. Some of these trends we miss because we are so accustomed to reading the text as we were taught by others, that we do not allow the text to speak for itself.

I wish I had a dollar for every time I have heard a preacher say that Saul gave up his Hebrew name, and took the name of Paul, when he became a Christian.[7] I have even heard eloquent sermons as to how *Saul* the persecutor fell down to earth, and up rose *Paul* the Christian, *Paul* the missionary, *Paul* the apostle.

It is very pretty, very traditional, and very inspiring. The only problem is that it isn't true. Read the book of Acts again. *Saul* meets the Lord on the way to Damascus. *Saul* gets up and goes into the city. Ananias is told to go visit *Saul*. *Saul* goes to Jerusalem. Barnabas meets *Saul*. Barnabas introduces *Saul* to the Twelve. *Saul* goes to Tarsus. *Saul* comes to Antioch. *Saul* is among the leaders of the church in Antioch. The Spirit tells the leaders of that church to set

Handwritten note: *Ex. of Paul crossing 2 cultures due to the change in his belief/religion. Saul → Paul in Act 13.*

aside Barnabas and *Saul* for a special task. B[a...] in their first missionary journey. . . . Then, a[...] Acts 13:9, Luke refers to "Saul, also known [...] point on, throughout the entire book of Act[...]

The fact of the matter is that Saul, like [...] had two names. One was the name in his tr[...] case, Judaism. He was named Saul after th[...] tribe of Benjamin. But he had also a Rom[...] outside of Jewish circles. That name wa[...] cultural *mestizo,* as were many of his cont[...]

As long as Saul/Paul is in a basically Jew[ish ...] refers to him as Saul. Now, as he begins his mission to the Gentiles, and at the precise moment when Saul is about to give his first witness before a Gentile, Luke, almost offhandedly, refers to "Saul, also known as Paul." If there is a difference between Saul and Paul, that difference does not revolve around the experience on the road to Damascus, but around the mission to the Gentiles. True, the two are connected. On the road to Damascus, before meeting the Lord, Saul, the proud Jew who has received the best Jewish education, is persecuting these false Jews who have allowed themselves to be led astray by heresy. They have been led to heresy, in part at least, because they are not real and strict Jews. They are Hellenists, people from the diaspora who have been influenced by pagan culture and customs, and who now are quite ready to embrace a new sect.

It has often been pointed out that this persecution of which the book Acts speaks is not against all Jewish Christians, but only against those Jewish Christians who are also of Hellenistic background, those who could not claim to be strict Jews, brought up in Palestine.

What we often miss (and I have already pointed out in chapter 1) is that it was other Hellenistic Jews who unleashed the persecution against Hellenistic Jewish Christians. In Acts 6:9 we are told that those who started the persecution by accusing Stephen were Hellenistic Jews: "Cyrenians, Alexandrians, and others of those from Cilicia and Asia." Apparently they were afraid that they too would be tainted by the accusation of heresy against Stephen and other Hellenists who had become Christian. Therefore, they made it very clear that they were true, strict Jews, and they did this by unleashing persecution against those from among their ranks who had become Christians.

Saul was from Cilicia. He too was a Hellenistic Jew. We do not know how long he had lived in Jerusalem. Still, he was known as Saul of Tarsus, and therefore as a Hellenistic Jew—one of those who did not quite belong, who were often suspect of not obeying the law as strictly as did the Jews from Jerusalem. (One even wonders if he might have been among those "from Cilicia" who, according to Acts 6:9, conspired to have Stephen brought before the Sanhedrin.) From the point of view of the good Jews in Jerusalem, Hellenistic Jews such as this Saul "of Tarsus" were cultural *mestizos* who constantly had to prove themselves to be true, pure, Orthodox Jews. Persecuting other Hellenistic Jews who had embraced "heterodoxy" such as Stephen was one of the ways in which these *mestizo* Jews could prove themselves to be true Jews.

"Saul" is a good Jewish name. It was the name of the first king of Israel, the great hero of the tribe of Benjamin. The man making his way from Jerusalem to Damascus, with letters authorizing him to initiate proceedings against any disciples that might be found there, must have been proud of his name. It was a good Jewish name; not a Greek one, such as Stephen. For a Jew from Tarsus, in faraway Cilicia, this must have been something to cling to—a badge of honor and of acceptance.

But that was some time ago. Now, in Acts 13, the path that began on the road to Damascus takes a new turn. Saul is now going on a mission to the Gentiles. Suddenly he finds himself facing a false prophet of Jewish origin, and standing before a Roman proconsul. This is the real beginning of his missionary career among the Gentiles. And it is precisely this moment, this beginning of his missionary career, that Luke chooses to let us know that this Saul is "also known as Paul."

Saul/Paul is part of that *mestizo* mass of the first century. Jewish, but not purely Jewish. A native of Tarsus, but also a Roman citizen. As a Jew, proud of his Jewish heritage; not quite ready to accept his

Hellenistic background. Actually, so eager to deny that background, that he was at least a consenting witness to the death of Stephen.

If the Alexandrines, Cyrenians, and people from Asia and Cilicia who set up the first persecution did so because they had to prove their true Jewish allegiance, one can imagine this Saul, from Tarsus in Cilicia, going to Damascus, "breathing threats and murder against the disciples of the Lord," and doing so because he was Saul, of the tribe of Benjamin, a true Jew, no matter what his connection with Tarsus and with the Hellenistic Diaspora.

What is happening in this thirteenth chapter of Acts is that Luke is telling us that in his mission to the Gentiles Saul came to terms with Paul, that he was able to claim his dual belonging—and therefore, in a certain sense, his own *mestizo* rootlessness. Furthermore, it is because Saul is also Paul, because the Jewish scholar is also capable of moving in Hellenistic and Roman circles, that he becomes the great apostle to the Gentiles.

That is a situation with which many Latinos can relate. I have a friend whose name is Jesse. At least, that is what his English-speaking friends call him. When he was born, he was baptized as "Jesús." But then he went to school. His teacher took a look at his name, and said, "You can't be Jesus!" So Jesús became Jesse. I have another friend, María Luisa, who is also Mary Lou. In another minority community, I have still another friend, Seung Lee, who is also Arthur Lee. Similarly, Saul was also Paul.

There have been times when Jesús has given up and simply called himself Jesse. So have María Luisa and Seung Lee. It is so painful not to belong! It is so painful to belong to two different worlds, and therefore to none! Latinos can easily understand this Jew from Tarsus, Saul, trying to prove to others, as well as to himself, that he was as good a Jew as any other, and therefore "breathing threats and murder against the disciples of the Lord."

The presence of *mestizaje,* as Elizondo correctly points out, is not a comfortable situation for the *mestizo,* nor for any of the two or more cultures that blend in the *mestizo.* That is why right now in the United States there are so many attempts to close the border, to have

The book of Acts is a cultural melting pot, where it shows the progressive change of the church & faith.

...ake certain that we are pure, to insist on the ... own particular culture.

...t such is not the way to the future. We know ...e world around us is changing. We know it, ...t we have been promised as Christians. We ...made Saul the great apostle to the Gentiles ...at Saul was also Paul; that the Jew was also ...the Greek-speaking Jew was also a Roman

...e that Paul can do what he does because he ...and that the entire book of Acts can be read as the progressive *mestizaje* of the church; **and** that the process and the goal of Christian mission may be interpreted as the progressive *mestizaje* of the church and the faith.

Mission, like *mestizaje,* takes place at the border, at the place of encounter. Significantly, in English we say "border," and in Spanish, *frontera*.[9] But when we translate the Spanish *frontera* back into English we can come up with either "border" or "frontier." In fact, commonly used Spanish has no equivalent to the English "frontier" as distinguished from "border."

This linguistic quirk, like many others, points to a different perception and a different historical reality. It was in 1492, slightly over five hundred years ago, that "Columbus sailed the ocean blue." In the centuries that followed, a veritable flood of humanity crossed the Atlantic and inundated these lands. (In fact, the flood was such that one could say that the conquest and colonization of the sixteenth to the nineteenth centuries were the continuation of the Germanic invasions that flooded the Roman Empire back in the fourth and fifth centuries.) These people came to conquer, to colonize, and to settle. They came to what they saw as a "frontier" in the English sense. They came to push back what they saw as darkness, to bring what they saw as civilization, to Christianize by means of the sword and the plow.

The encounter was equally brutal, devastating, and inhumane in the Spanish colonies and in the English colonies; but there was an important difference. The lands that the Spanish conquered south of

Texas were densely populated. Their original inhabitants had organized themselves into empires whose wealth was fabulous by any standards. Even had they wished to do so, the Spanish could never have simply swept the Indians aside and occupied their lands. But they had no wish to do so, for the value of the land was precisely in the native population that could be forced to work and mine it. The Spanish wanted little to do with the Indians as human beings. They even debated if the Indians had souls. But they could not dispense with them. Meanwhile, some time after the conquest of Mexico and Peru, the British began to settle in North America. They too came to the frontier. They too saw themselves as bringing light and faith and civilization to a new land. So, just as ruthlessly and as brutally as the Spanish were doing in the south, the British in the north set out to create a new empire. If there was Nueva España in the south, there was New England in the north; and if there was Nuevo León in the south, there was New Hampshire in the north. The difference was that in the north it was possible and convenient to push back the native inhabitants rather than to conquer and subdue them. What northern colonialists wanted was land. The original inhabitants were a hindrance. So, instead of subjugating the Indians, they set about to push them off their lands, and eventually to exterminate them. If the myth in the Spanish colonies was that the Indians were like children who needed someone to govern them, the myth in the English colonies was that the Indians were nonpeople; they didn't exist, their lands were a vacuum. In north Georgia, in the middle of Cherokee County, there is a monument to a white man who was, so the monument says, "the first man to settle in these parts." And this, in a county that is still called "Cherokee"!

This contrast in the colonizing process led to a "border" mentality in Mexico and much of Latin America, and a "frontier" mentality in the United States. Because the Spanish colonizers were forced to live with the original inhabitants of the land, a *mestizo* population and culture developed. Eventually, a new reality was born and acknowledged as part of the central mythology of the new culture. Today, in a plaza in Mexico City, which marks the place of the last great armed struggle between the Aztecs and the Spanish, there is a marker that attempts to explain what took place there: "There were neither victors nor vanquished; it was rather the painful birth of the new race which is the Mexican people." Significantly, the square itself is called the "Plaza de las Tres Culturas"—the Plaza of Three Cultures. This is too rosy a picture, for the Aztecs were indeed vanquished, and for many generations had to pay dearly for it. Nevertheless, it is true that from that moment the true growing edge of Mexican life was not the geographical frontier, but rather the other less discernible though equally real border at which people of different cultures thrown together by history met, clashed, rebelled, intermarried, and eventually produced a new, *mestizo* reality. In contrast, in the lands to the north, the process and the myth were of a constantly moving frontier, pushing back the native inhabitants of the land, interacting with them as little as possible. There was civilization this side of the frontier; and a void at the other side. The West was to be "won." The western line, the frontier, was seen as the growing edge; but it was expected to produce growth by mere expansion rather than by interaction.

Early in the nineteenth century, the western frontier of the United States met the Mexican border. The frontier could not be stopped. It had developed into the mythology of a Manifest Destiny and a foreign policy to reach the other ocean. The result was war, first in Texas and then in the very heartland of Mexico. It was arguably the most unjustifiable, unjust, and despicable war this nation has ever waged. The result is the border of today. We do well to remember that the border was established by force, lest we take it to be as God-given as the Rio Grande.

The main point is that there is a vast difference between a border and a frontier. A frontier is by definition unidirectional. It can only move ahead. Anything moving back across it is an incursion of the forces of evil and backwardness into the realm of light and progress. A border, in contrast, is by definition bidirectional. A border is the place at which two realities, two worldviews, two cultures, meet and interact. Both the frontier and the border are growing edges. But at the frontier growth takes place by conquest, by pushing the adversary back, while at the border growth takes place by encounter, by mutual enrichment. A true border, a true place of encounter, is by nature permeable. It is not like medieval armor, but rather like skin. Our skin does set a limit to where our body begins and where it ends. Our skin also sets certain limits to our give-and-take with our environment, keeping out certain germs, helping us to select that in our environment which we are ready to absorb. But if we ever close up our skin, we die.

Just as the "frontera" may be interpreted as "frontier" or as "border," so can mission proceed according to these two very different models. Traditionally, we have read the history of Christian mission in terms of frontier rather than border, of conquest rather than *mestizaje*. In chapter 1 we have already seen that it is possible to read Acts, not in the traditionally triumphalistic way, but rather as the conversion of Christianity—or, as we would say now, as the story of the growth of Christianity at its borders, which are not only geographical, but also cultural. According to the traditional reading, what Acts tells is the story of the geographical advance of the church, constantly pushing the frontier, from Jerusalem throughout Judea, and then Samaria, and eventually "to the ends of the earth" (Acts 1:8). That may well be true; but it is only part of the story. The other part is that practically every step of expansion can also be seen as a further conversion—in other words, that the church's growing edge, rather than an impermeable frontier that simply advances, is more like a border, in which advance also implies learning from the new context—one might even say that the mission progresses, not by conquest nor by simple, direct expansion, but rather by *mestizaje*.

The contrast between the border and the frontier mind-sets appears in various places in the Bible, sometimes quite unexpectedly. The most unexpected place is probably the book of Joshua, noted for its unrelenting destruction of the original inhabitants of Canaan, and often taken as a guide and justification for the destruction of the original inhabitants of this hemisphere. Yet even in that book Hispanic scholar Francisco García-Treto finds a significant undertone of what I have called the "border" approach, or what Elizondo would call *mestizaje*.

García-Treto begins by acknowledging that there is much in the Bible and in its interpretation that can be and has been used in rather oppressive ways. He then moves on to agree with a number of contemporary scholars that the story of the conquest of Canaan as told in the Deuteronomic history is greatly shaped by the struggle against Canaanite religion and culture at the time when the telling of the history itself was taking shape. At that point, deuteronomic theology sought to support religious and cultural purity by claiming that the land had been conquered on the basis of a covenant that required purity. This is clearly spelled out in Deut. 20:16-18:

> But as for the towns of these peoples that the LORD your God is giving you as an inheritance, you must not let anything that breathes remain alive. You shall annihilate them . . . just as the LORD your God has commanded, so that they may not teach you to do all the abhorrent things that they do for their gods, and you thus sin against the LORD your God.

García-Treto acknowledges that this understanding of the covenant as requiring genocide is part of the biblical record, and has often served as a justification for similar genocidal actions and ideologies. But he reminds us that the supposedly marked contrast between the Hebrews and the Canaanites is supported by little or no archaeological evidence, thus suggesting that the contrast itself was part of the deuteronomic rereading of history. He then points out that, underlying the official history that supports the strict deuteronomic "ban" on the original inhabitants of the land, there are indications in the biblical record of another side to the same story—a side that shows that the ban was not as strict as the deuteronomist historian suggests.

As a case in point, he focuses on the story of the Gibeonites in Joshua 9, claiming that "the discourse of the Bible is in Joshua 9, as in many other places, conflicted discourse, discourse which betrays by its moments of embarrassment the gap between ideology and praxis."[11] At this point, he agrees with Dana Nolan Fewell, who argues that there are a number of stories in Joshua where "fluid identity boundaries render nationalistic categories ambivalent and call into question the obsession with annihilating outsiders."[12] To this he adds some reflections and punctualizations to Susan Niditch's study on the theme of the underdog and the trickster in biblical tradition,[13] which he then enriches with references to the parallelisms with some of the famous folkloric tricksters of the Americas: Annancy, Brer Rabbit, Coyote, and the trickster of the Hispanic Southwest, Pedro Urdemalas.

The point is that the Gibeonites, who according to the deuteronomic ideology should have been killed, manage to survive by trickery, "by stealing the covenant, much as the patriarch [Jacob] had stolen the blessing."[14] Surprisingly, Yahweh accepts the trickery of the Gibeonites, just as Isaac, and Yahweh with him, had accepted the trickery of Jacob. The result is beneficial not only for the Gibeonites, but also for Israel:

> The covenant has been changed by the challenge: while on the one hand the survivals of the Gibeonites—and of others, notably Rahab and her family—are indeed subversions of the prophetic ideal of an exclusive covenant between Yahweh and *his* people, it is on the other an extension of that covenant toward an inclusive vision which would save the god of Joshua from merciless despotism, and the people of that god from unspeakable inhumanity.[15]

In all of this, one can see the theme of the *mestizo,* and how that experience parallels what García-Treto finds in this text. The *mestizo,* like the Gibeonite, must fight for survival, for the very right to exist. But that fight cannot be waged frontally, for this would lead to annihilation. Therefore, the *mestizo,* like the Gibeonites, like Brer Rabbit, Coyote, and Pedro Urdemalas, must find a course of action where wisdom takes the form of wiliness—which is part of the reason why the stereotype of the *mestizo* includes craftiness. Having won survival, however, the *mestizo,* like the Gibeonite, still does not attain equality—the *mestizos* are still expected, like the Gibeonites, to be "hewers of wood and drawers of water for the congregation."

Another story that becomes particularly interesting when read from the perspective of *mestizaje* and *mulatez* is the account of Queen Esther. Loida Martell-Otero correctly points out that we usually read the book of Esther as if Mordecai were the good uncle who leads Esther along paths of justice. But what the book actually says is that Mordecai practically "sells" the child he is supposed to protect, and who obeys him implicitly (Esther 2:20). Mordecai instructs her "to pass," hiding her Jewish identity (Esther 2:10, 20). Meanwhile Mordecai himself sits "at the king's gate"—that is, is a lesser courtier seeking the king's favor. Martell-Otero goes on:

> And as all marginalized people who sell out, he has a false sense of pride that endangers all his people. Instead of taking responsibility for that, he lays the responsibility of seeking a solution on his niece. Esther, on the other hand, obeys as a woman. She too has to play the game. But once confronted with the danger she is in, confronted with the fact that even when you obey and play by the rules you still die, there is a *kairos* moment, a conversion for her. She comes into full personhood. It is at that point that the narration changes. She no longer behaves as Esther, but as *Queen Esther*; no longer taking orders, but giving them; no longer passive, but taking the initiative.[16]

Although not a *mestiza* in the physical sense, Esther is culturally *mestiza*. She is a Jew, but tries to pass as one who is not. She lives in the king's palace, and yet her roots are not there. Her roots are among the Jewish people, and yet the very Jew who has authority over her conspires to have her hide her Jewish identity. And, like the Gibeonites and others who must survive by their wits, she too is wily.

Mestizaje, both genetic and cultural, is part of the biblical reality, even though the deuteronomist historian may have tried to suppress it. In writing his Gospel, Matthew could well have tried to suppress Jesus' own *mestizaje*—he was, after all, the "son of David" come to claim David's throne. Instead, of the four women mentioned in his genealogy, two are Gentiles. Therefore, as followers of the *mestizo* Jesus, we shall learn to read the Bible, and life itself, as *mestizos* who have much to offer to the false purities claimed by today's deuteronomists!

CHAPTER FOUR

Exiles and Aliens

A fourth paradigm that helps explain how Hispanics read the Scripture is exile and alienness. For many of our cousins in Latin America the Exodus becomes the central paradigm; for many of us in the United States that function belongs to the Babylonian exile. For whatever reasons, we find ourselves in a land not our own—in some cases, in a land that was our own but is no longer. In that land, we must find a way to live, to survive, and to be faithful.

Exile implies a strange sort of marginalization. In exile, one leaves what has been the center of one's life and moves to the periphery. Most often, the first stage in the process has been a decay in that center. Such decay may have—and usually has—a variety of causes: outside invasion or intervention, civil strife, economic disorder and decline, or economic and political oppression. No matter what the reason, the land that our eyes first saw can no longer sustain the life of peace and joy that God intends. As we look back to those lands, many of us can say with the prophet:

> We get our bread at the peril of our lives,
>   because of the sword in the wilderness.
> Our skin is black as an oven

from the scorching heat of famine.
Women are raped in Zion,
   virgins in the towns of Judah.
Princes are hung up by their hands;
   no respect is shown to the elders.
Young men are compelled to grind,
   and boys stagger under loads of wood.
The old men have left the city gate,
   the young men their music.
The joy of our hearts has ceased;
   our dancing has been turned to mourning. (Lam. 5:9-15)

Thus, exiles come from old centers that no longer hold to new centers—sometimes, as in the case of the Babylonian exiles, to new centers that are at least partly responsible for the destruction of the old.

We have come to the center, yet we remain at the periphery. In a way, we no longer know where the center is—for that is the very nature of exile, a life in which one is forced to revolve around a center that is not one's own, and that in many ways one does not wish to own. Exile is a dislocation of the center, with all the ambiguities and ambivalence of such dislocation. Thus the exiled poet sings about not singing:

By the rivers of Babylon—
   there we sat down and there we wept
   when we remembered Zion.
On the willows there
   we hung up our harps.
How could we sing the LORD's song
   in a foreign land? (Ps. 137:1-2, 4)

This experience of dislocation of the center, of being at the periphery revolving around a center that is not our own, is a common Latino experience—even for many who have not come to this land as exiles, but were born here. In general, people of the dominant culture who are left out for reasons of class or education look to the center for meaning and leadership, and dream of moving closer to the center. In contrast, many Latinos, even those who were born here and those whose ancestors have lived in this country for generations, have little or no desire to move toward the center, for they fear that the cost will be a loss of identity. Therefore, even in the case of some of the Hispanos of Nuevo Mexico, whose ancestors were in the land before it was taken over by the United States, exile becomes a viable paradigm for the interpretation of the Scripture and of life.

It is important to underscore that the category of exile and alienness applies, not only to those who were born in other lands and have migrated to the United States, but also to many in the second, third, and fourth generations. According to census figures, roughly three-fourths of all Latinos in the United States are American citizens by birth. Yet they too have to deal with issues of exile and alienness. The very fact that the common perception is that most Hispanics are recent immigrants, means that even those who were born here are often made to feel as if they are newcomers. You apply for a job, and your papers are scrutinized with particular care just because you look different. You take any form of public transportation north from the borderlands, and if you are not very well dressed you may well be asked for your papers. Furthermore, since there is constant coming and going to and from the lands of our ancestors, many of us keep close emotional contacts with those lands, even though we may never have lived there. And, since many of us live in lands where our culture has deep historical roots—especially in the Southwest—there is also a sense of being aliens in our own lands.

This may be seen in all sorts of details of our daily life. For instance, one of the most popular Mexican-American restaurants in San Antonio is called *Mi Tierra*—My Land. This is a significantly ambiguous name, which may be understood both as a nostalgic remembrance of *mi tierra* south of the border, or as a claim that this land, even though invaded and taken over by others, is still *mi tierra*.

This is why Hispanic theology in the United States, from its very inception, has been concerned with issues of migration, exile, and alienness. Thus, in one of the earliest articles in *Apuntes*, Francisco O. García-Treto, of Trinity University in San Antonio, analyzed the significance of the *alien* (in Hebrew, *ger*) in the Old Testament, and sought to relate it to the Hispanic situation in the United States.

Taking his cue from Psalm 146:9, "The LORD watches over the strangers," and studying a series of texts in which the term *ger* appears, García-Treto declares that:

> If we were to summarize in a single phrase the clear thesis of these biblical traditions, it would be, simply, that the *ger* is protected by Yahweh. This ancient Hebrew tradition is clearly different from the xenophobic attitudes that were prevalent in antiquity. . . . The *ger,* the alien who lives among the people of Israel, could have been completely deprived of dignity and even of the most basic right to justice, since the *ger* lacked the two traditional elements that, at the purely human level, were the foundation of dignity and right in Israel: hereditary property, and the protection of family and kinship. The biblical tradition, however, surprises us by including the *ger* as the object of a particular predilection on Yahweh's part, and therefore to be included, jointly with the native, in the rites that expressed the community's solidarity, as well as among those to whom the law grants a special protection.[1]

This is not merely an act of charity on the part of Israel. It is grounded on the law of Yahweh, with the consequence that the *ger,* just as the widow, the orphan, the poor, and the Levite, has the undeniable right to those systems of protection established for those who do not have tenure of land. Furthermore, the *ger* even serves a specific religious function in Israel, reminding the people that Israel too was alien in the land of Egypt, and remains forever alien in a land that ultimately belongs only to God. García-Treto continues:

> The biblical tradition . . . reiterates that Israel not only was, but still is, an "alien" people. Solidarity with the dispossessed is not only an external attitude, but the deepest reality of Israel's existence as people of Yahweh. References such as Deuteronomy 28:8 remind Israel that it too was a *ger* in Egypt; but even more relevant are others such as the one in Leviticus 25:23, where Yahweh admonishes the people: "The land shall not be sold in perpetuity, for the land is mine; with me you are but aliens and tenants."[2]

García-Treto then goes on to claim that it was this "paradoxical concept" that the people of Yahweh are aliens even in their possession of the promised land, that made it possible for Israel to survive the Babylonian exile, and later the Roman conquest and eventual loss of the land. Thus, Israel survived because the aliens among them had been a constant reminder that they too were aliens, and that therefore, important as the land was, their existence as a people did not depend on its possession.

Significantly, in the very next issue of *Apuntes* Jorge Lara-Braud published an article in which, quite independently from García-Treto and in this case from a largely autobiographical perspective, he came to similar conclusions with regard to the role of Hispanics in the United States.[3] Taking care not to fall into the common trap of confusing the United States with the Promised Land, or its people with Israel, Lara-Braud points out two contradictory currents that have been formative for North American consciousness: on the one hand, the "myths of origin" that describe the "primordial community" as immigrants from Northern Europe, and in particular from Britain; on the other, the dream of "a nation that would welcome all those whom other societies reject." It is in this second aspect of the myths of origin, often drowned in nativistic waves, that Lara-Braud sees hope for this nation:

> From the beginning it was taken for granted that there would be a permanent renewal of society, because this nation had entered a covenant with God, and that covenant required a constant conversion and reconversion. I really believe that without taking this into account regarding the North American subconsciousness, it is impossible to show what a blessing immigrants can continue being. . . . I wish I could once again convince North Americans that every time an immigrant reaches this nation, the dream of the birth of an exemplary society gains renewed strength.[4]

If this is true, it means that aliens must no longer be seen as people who come to these lands in order to draw benefits from them, but also to bless and improve them. More important, it means that those of us who have come from other lands, as well as those who were born here but are still seen as aliens, can look at ourselves in a different way. We are not mere "takers," who benefit from the freedom and the economic opportunities available in this country. We are also "givers," who bring enhanced meaning to freedom, and who also contribute significantly to the economic well-being of the whole. This self-consciousness is crucial for the welfare of the entire community, for as long as we see ourselves as being here only under sufferance, and not as active participants in future building, much of our potential contribution will be lost.

A biblical point of reference that immediately comes to mind when we think of alienness in these terms is the story of Joseph in Egypt. Joseph himself—like so many of us—did not have a very clear idea why he was in Egypt. Yet it turns out that he was there for the salvation both of Egypt and of his own original people. Had Egypt not been able to discover and utilize Joseph's gifts, Egypt would have suffered grave loss along with Israel and with Joseph. Had Joseph remained quiet and submissive, allowing himself to be seduced by Potiphar's wife, or telling the Pharaoh what he wanted to hear, both Joseph and Egypt would have also suffered great loss. It took a Joseph who was willing to use his gifts, even when it meant speaking a word that the Pharaoh would rather not hear, as well as a Pharaoh who was willing to accept and to use the gifts of an alien slave to avert the threatening famine.

Clearly, the reason why the dominant culture does not see this in the story is that there is a dislocation on where that community sees itself in the narrative. Since Joseph is the hero of the story, we good Christians must be the Josephs of today's story. There is some value in such an interpretation, which would mean that Christians should use their vision and their gifts for the welfare of the society around us. But there is another dimension that is forgotten when that is all we see in the story. It is possible that those doing the interpretation, if they are the religious and social leaders of our day—people well placed in the dominant society—should read the story placing themselves, not in the sandals of Joseph, but rather in the shoes of the Pharaoh. In that case, the text no longer speaks so much about how good Christians ought to try to influence the powerful, but rather about how the powerful—particularly if they seek to do the will of God—must seek the alien, discover their gifts, and seek whatever wisdom and guidance those gifts might offer. Remember: Joseph will eventually save his own household; but in the process he will also save Egypt!

Another biblical narrative that gains particular significance when read from the point of view of the exile and the alien is the story of Ruth and Naomi. The story of Naomi is similar to that of many Latino women who come to this land following a husband whom they then lose to either death or divorce. Naomi has a line of connection with her ancient home in her two sons. As we can see from the rest of the story, that is the only thing that keeps her in Moab. As Latinos, many of us can empathize with Naomi, for we are often torn between yearning for distant lands and love for our immediate community. When her two sons die, the story tells us, "the woman was left without her two sons and her husband" (Ruth 1:5). There was no longer anything to tie her to her adoptive land—a land that had not treated her well—and she began considering their return. Still, there were bonds that she had established with her Moabite daughters-in-law, and the scene of her parting with Orpah has dimensions of tenderness that we often miss because we allow Ruth's faithfulness to eclipse Orpah's love. The result of Ruth's fidelity to her mother-in-law is that it is now her turn to be an alien. Boaz recognizes the value and the daring of her actions: "how you left your father and mother and your native land and came to a people that you did not know before" (Ruth 2:11). This is not just a story of two women following each other from Moab to Bethlehem. It is the story of a woman who becomes an alien for the sake of her husband, and another woman who becomes an alien for the sake of her mother-in-law. It is a story of belonging in the midst of not belonging. It is, in short, a story of exile and alienness.

The biblical writer, however, does not stop there. We are told that this story of exile and alienness becomes central in the history of Israel, for Ruth had a son by Boaz, and "they named him Obed; he became the father of Jesse, the father of David" (Ruth 4:17). In other words, the alien who followed Naomi to Bethlehem became the great-grandmother of the great king of Israel! And this is a fact not lost on the gospel writer, whose genealogy of the Messiah lists Ruth by name (Matt. 1:5).

On this score, however, it is not only Egypt that has to think differently about Joseph and Israel that has to think differently about the Moabite; it is also the aliens who have to think differently about themselves. The experience of an exile community that is merely tolerated—or that is welcomed at first, and then resented—can easily lead to an escapism in which one lives only for the time of return, or for the time when we shall enjoy life eternal, without the blemishes and the pains of this earthly life.

This process is quite evident in the Latino community in the United States. One of the most popular songs during the early years of the Cuban exile told of how *"cuando salí de Cuba, dejé enterrado mi corazón"*—when I left Cuba I left my heart buried there. A popular Puerto Rican song speaks of having to leave Old San Juan, *"pues lo quiso el destino"*—for destiny willed it. Then it goes on to affirm, much like the Cuban song, *"pero mi corazón se quedó frente al mar, en mi viejo San Juan"*—but my heart remained facing the sea, in my old San Juan. For years, Cubans in South Florida refused to participate in local affairs and in the political process, for they were awaiting a prompt return to their island. When they now participate in politics, they often do so, not in the light of issues in Florida or in the United States, but in the light of what a particular politician says about Cuba and Castro—even when the politician in question is running for a position such as the state legislature, which has nothing to do with foreign policy. And it has often been said that Puerto Ricans can live thirty years in New York without psychologically unpacking their suitcases. Thus, the hope of an imminent return leads to a practical escapism, in which one lives life, so to speak, between parentheses.

When such dreams of return from exile do not materialize, they are often transmuted into another sort of escapism, best illustrated by popular hymns such as *"soy peregrino aquí, mi hogar lejano está"*—I am but a pilgrim here, my home is far away. At this point, one no longer hopes for a return to a material homeland, but rather for escape from this world, all of which has become a land of exile, into the heavenly spiritual mansions. Again, this leads to a life lived between parentheses, as if most of what takes place in the present were of no ultimate significance.

At this point one is reminded of Jewish apocalypticism, which developed out of a similar hope of return to a time when Israel was the center of her own life. When such hopes failed to materialize, they were often transmuted into an otherworldliness that eventually became one of the many streams contributing to gnosticism.[5]

The point here is that the marginalization that goes with an experience of exile can easily be compounded when a people in exile accept their marginalization on the grounds that their exile will not last long, that this is just a temporary situation that will soon pass. As Latinos, very often we have ignored the political issues of this land, forgetting that, marginal though we might be, in the welfare of the land we too shall find our welfare.

For that reason, as Jorge González forcefully pointed out to our group, Jeremiah's letter to the exiles in Babylon is of the greatest significance for us:

> Build houses and live in them; plant gardens and eat what they produce. . . . But seek the welfare of the city where I have sent you into exile, and pray to the LORD on its behalf, for in its welfare you will find your welfare.　　　　　　　　　　　　　　　　　(Jer. 29: 5, 7)

Most particularly, we must remember that those who announced an early return from exile were declared to be false prophets:

> Do not let the prophets and the diviners who are among you deceive you, and do not listen to the dreams that they dream, for it is a lie that they are prophesying to you in my name; I did not send them, says the LORD.　　　　　　　　　　　　　　　　　　　　　　(Jer. 29:8-9)

Also significantly, Eldin Villafañe's new book, dealing with urban ministry from a Latino perspective, draws its title from the same passage: *Seek the Welfare of the City*.[6] Villafañe, who has extensive experience as a Pentecostal minister, educator, and organizer in the Latino barrios of the Northeast, says that Jeremiah's:

words to the Exile in Babylon are still relevant. As against the false prophets who might call for "assimilation," "revolution," or "escapism," Jeremiah calls for "critical engagement"—for presence.[7]

Still, the urge to return is always strong, and thus it is also Jorge González who points out that Jeremiah, who will have to announce exile and eventually himself go into exile, was in a sense a returnee from exile:

> How the world turns! The descendants of Eli, who was Yahweh's priest at Shiloh, were expelled from Jerusalem and forced to live in Anathoth. In 1 Kings 2:26-27 this deportation is seen as the fulfillment of the curse on Eli's descendants that was announced in 1 Samuel 2:27-36. Now Jeremiah, a descendant of Abiathar, the priest whom Solomon deported, returns to the very Temple from which his family had been expelled, and it is precisely in that place that he will proclaim his message.[8]

Significantly, the interpreter who wrote these words and noticed the irony in the history of Jeremiah's family is a Cuban exile himself with ancestors who went to Cuba as exiles from Appalachicola when Florida became British. The irony in Jeremiah's story would not be lost on one whose family history is similarly ironic!

This need to claim permanence while in exile may be seen in a sermon preached to an assembly of Hispanic leaders from all over the nation, where the theme was the need to begin writing our own history. The preacher related the writing of our history to the raising of the monument in Gilgal after the crossing of the Jordan. He said:

> Raising a monument is a remembrance of the past; but it is also a promise for the future. Certainly, the crossing of the Red Sea was much more remarkable than the crossing of the Jordan. Yet, the people of Israel raise a monument after crossing the Jordan, and not after crossing the Red Sea. Why? Because what comes after the Red Sea is the desert, a place of passage, a place of transition, a land of landless and rootless nomads. But what comes after Jordan is the Promised Land, a place of permanence, a place for planting vineyards and growing roots, a place where the children of Israel, and their children,

and their children in turn, will live. This is why upon raising the monument Joshua says to his followers: "When your children shall ask their parents . . . ," that is to say, that our children will live here; that in this land we shall set out roots; that this is no longer a desert for wandering about, but a land for construction. The monument at Gilgal, while remembering the past, also promises a future: "When your children shall ask their parents *in time to come. . . .*" The monument does not say only "Here we are," but also "Here we shall be."[9]

For this preacher, however, as for much of the Hispanic community, this does not mean that things will become easier as soon as we decide to settle. On the contrary, the very decision to settle, and even to "seek the welfare of the city," brings about more opposition and even a greater sense of alienness. Thus, after quoting the passage in which we are told that the people of Canaan were filled with fear when they heard that the Israelites had crossed the Jordan, he remarked:

I know not whether there was a spy from the inhabitants of the land looking upon what the people of Israel did and what Joshua said. But if there was, these actions and words would have caused him to panic: these people not only have crossed the river, but have come to stay! They have put up a monument for their descendants to remember this day! They expect their descendants to be here still!

Likewise, when today we begin to speak about leaving a remembrance for our children, and for their children in turn, we are proclaiming to the world that we are here to stay. Perhaps not all of us have crossed the river dry-shod—or dry backed! But no matter how we came here, we are here to stay!

I can imagine that spy from Jericho running back to his city. "We are much bigger than they—so much so, that next to us they look like grasshoppers. But these people have come to stay! Build the walls higher! Close the gates! Call up the army!"

Or, if it were today, I can imagine the same panic: "Close the border! Call the Migra! Require them to have work permits! Apply Proposition 187! These people are here to stay. They are talking about writing their history, about raising a monument for their children, and for their children's children."[10]

This preacher was careful then to avoid confusing the United States with the Promised Land, by pointing out that as Christians we are still pilgrims. Yet it is clear that what he was trying to do in this sermon was to insist on the need to "seek the welfare of the city," to grow roots in the land, even though it is a land that still treats us as aliens and exiles.

CHAPTER FIVE

Solidarity

The paradigms we have studied so far—marginality, poverty, mestizaje, and exile/aliennness—all sound rather negative. Although they are valuable in that they contribute to our understanding of the Scriptures, and may also give us significant insights into issues that others simply do not see, they are not pleasant experiences. One could say that they are not only paradigms for biblical interpretation, but also paradigms for how we understand and experience sin and its consequences.

Yet, the Bible is essentially about good news. It is about good news that overcomes evil. In our case, it is about good news in the context of marginality, poverty, and so on. Therefore, if we have all of these paradigms that help us understand evil and its workings, we must also have paradigms that help us understand and experience redemption. Obviously, as Hispanic Christians we employ many of the images and paradigms that the church has always used to express its experience of redemption: grace, salvation, being found, life eternal, and new birth. But also for many of us there is a particular paradigm that expresses an important element in the good news that is the gospel. That paradigm is solidarity, often expressed in terms such as "family" and "community."

As a person who has repeatedly experienced alienness, Pablo Jiménez reads the story of Abraham in an illuminating way. For him, the call to Abraham, "Go from your country and your kindred and your father's house to the land that I will show you" (Gen. 12:1), is a call to become an alien, a foreigner, a homeless person. When Abraham comes to "the land that I will show you," he will do so as an alien, and therefore he and his people must forever remember and understand the alien. One may see a connection between this and the manner in which the Old Testament repeatedly understands Israel's experience of slavery and alienness: "You shall not wrong or oppress a resident alien, for you were aliens in the land of Egypt" (Exod. 22:21). "You shall love the alien as yourself, for you were aliens in the land of Egypt" (Lev. 19:34).

Jiménez, however, takes the theme in a slightly different direction, relating Abraham's alienness to that of the early Christians addressed in 1 Peter: "the exiles of the Dispersion" (1 Pet. 1:1). He then shows that the good news in 1 Peter is precisely this: a "spiritual house" for the homeless (1 Pet. 2:5); a "chosen race" for those with no family; a "holy nation" for those with no country (1 Pet. 2:9). Thus, following John Elliott's theme of 1 Peter as offering "a home for the homeless,"[1] Jiménez relates this to the sense of homelessness and uprootedness that is common to the Latino experience. Then, he parallels the theme of remembrance in the texts quoted above from Exodus and Leviticus, insisting that, if we have a place in our churches, it is because they are a home for the alien, and that therefore our churches must be a welcoming home for those who have no home and a family for all those who have no functional family. At this point Jiménez reminds us that 1 Peter is not just about homeless aliens, but also about:

A "spiritual house" (2:5) for the homeless.
A "chosen race" (2:9) for those who have no kindred.
A "holy nation" (2:9) for those who are without a country.

Note that in these three points what stands out is a structure of solidarity for those whose essential experience is of rootlessness and alienation: a house or family, a race, and a nation are all terms of solidarity.

This leads us to consider the theme of the family. One of the manners in which Latinos experience alienation and exile is in the loss of the extended family. For us, exile means the loss, not only of familiar places and land, but also of family. This is true even when we have traveled with our nuclear family. Those of us who grew up in other lands frequently bring with us an experience and understanding of "family" that is quite different from the nuclear family that is so romanticized, and whose demise is so deplored in North American society. The same is true of those of us who grew up in this country, in areas where our own ancestors had also lived for generations. For us, "family" is not only the parents and their children, but also grandparents, aunts, uncles, cousins, nephews, nieces, and others. In the rural areas in which many grew up, most of these relatives lived in the same valley or community. Even in cities, many of us come from an experience where there were always relatives around or nearby.

On the other hand, those of us who have grown up in "exile"—second or later generation Latinos—have often lost touch with that extended family. There is still the pull of such a family, for it is deeply ingrained in our culture. Thus, we often live in a tension between what we understand family to be—an extended family—and the reality we experience—in the best of cases, a relatively small nuclear family.

The function of the extended family is much more than providing a pleasant, somewhat quaint experience of security and love. The present notion of the nuclear family is a relatively recent phenomenon, mostly the result of the industrial revolution and of developments that took place since then. During most of human history, the "normal" family has been the extended family. The nuclear family, so romanticized by movies about the fifties and so mourned by Christians who promote "family values," is not the "normal" family. In fact, there is much to indicate that the nuclear family, far from being the quintessential family, is merely a temporary stage between the extended family and the final dissolution of the family—in other words, that the nuclear family, far from being the ideal, may already be part of the problem.

On this score, think of the psychological role of the family in the formation of the individual psyche, as studied by Freud and by so many after him. When we realize that the family relations that Freud studied as normative were in fact a recent development, one begins to wonder whether the problems that Freud discovered did not already have to do with the dissolution of the family, even in those families that were then considered strong and viable. Think for instance of the pressures put on the father of a modern nuclear family, to be the sole—or almost the sole—male role for his children. Or think of the similar pressures put on the mother of such a family. Little wonder that so many fail! Little wonder that, fearing failure, so many abandon their families altogether!

Then compare that with the manner in which male and female role models exist and develop in an extended family. In such a family, the father does not have to be a perfect role model for his children, who have other alternative models in uncles, grandfathers, and cousins. Likewise, if the mother fails in her role—even if she fails only partially—there are many others to fill the gap. Furthermore, such "failures" on the part of parents are not even perceived as such, for there is no need nor expectation that the parents meet every demand placed on them as role models. That is the normal function, not only of parents, but of the entire extended family.

For many of us, the most painful aspect of the experience of exile and alienness is the loss of the extended family—or, more precisely, of the family in its fuller sense. This is parallel to the loss of community, since for us the two are closely entwined. Actually, since "family" encompasses all relatives, including those by marriage, the lines between "family" and "community" cannot be sharply drawn. Presbyterian pastor Jill Martínez has clearly seen this connection:

> Understanding the community as family has been a way of life for the Hispanic. The Hispanic has traditionally understood this reality of "la comunidad y la familia"; they are interchangeable where service and work are tied together. Each person is brought into the close life of

friends and family as he/she serves in the community for the good of the whole family. As the bonds of trust are established through these relationships, the person becomes a part of the family fully sharing in the work and in the celebrations of the community.[2]

One of the points at which all of this impacts our biblical interpretation most directly is in texts having to do with the church as the household or family of God. Look for instance at Ephesians 2:19, where alienness is contrasted with belonging to the family of God: "So then you are no longer strangers and aliens, but you are citizens with the saints and also members of the household of God." For most people in the dominant community, this is a beautiful image. For most in the Hispanic and other uprooted communities, it is an existential experience.

Look again at that text, and think of the original condition of most who became Christians when this epistle was written. In the Roman Empire that so dazzles our imagination, the vast majority of the population, particularly in the cities, were a mass of people with few roots or rights. Rights were defined by one's status in relation to the city—in other words, by one's citizenship. In contrast to the way we use that term today, most people had no "citizenship," for being a citizen required much more than mere legal residence in a city. It required a certain standing in that city—and it also required having such standing in a city that had the right to grant "citizenship." Paul was a citizen of both Tarsus (Acts 21:39) and Rome (Acts 16:37; 22:25-29; 23:27); but most early Christians had no citizenship. Still, the Epistle says that its readers were worse than noncitizens: they were "strangers" (*xenoi*), meaning that they did not even have the normal connections that gave residents of a city their own sense of belonging. Slaves, freed men and women, and various others drew their status in a city from the citizen to whom they belonged or whom they honored as a patron. But "strangers" had no such connections. No matter how long they lived in a city, they were worse than other noncitizens.

Furthermore, these people were not only strangers; they were also "aliens." This is the NRSV's rendering of the Greek term *paroikoi,* the same word that appears also in 1 Peter, where it was taken as a reference to homelessness. The *paroikos* is one who has no fixed *oikia*—home or house. Thus, in putting these two words together, Ephesians depicts the earlier life of its readers as one of exile and alienness. They had no citizenship, nor even the rights that most people would derive from other citizens. They had no home. They were, as the NRSV puts it, "strangers and aliens"—or, in what would probably be a better translation, homeless foreigners.

To such people, the gospel could hardly be put in more powerful terms than in this one verse in Ephesians. They who were not even second-class citizens, but *xenoi,* are now *citizens* with the saints. And they who had no home, but were *paroikoi,* now are *members of the household [oikeioi] of God.* The stranger with no rights is now a citizen; the homeless wanderer is now part of the family of God! Note that here, as in the case of Hispanics, there is a connection between community and family, between being a citizen and being a member of the family.

Transferring all of this to the twentieth century and to the condition of Hispanics in the United States, the parallelisms are quite clear. Although many of us have reason to complain that in many ways we are "second-class citizens," the truth is that many of us are not citizens at all: noncitizens of the United States for lack of proper documentation, and noncitizens of our countries of origin because in many cases they are countries where the very rights of citizenship are repeatedly and easily trampled. And we are also "homeless aliens" (*paroikoi*), not necessarily in the sense of not having physical shelter, but certainly in the sense of not having a "household," a "family" such as Jill Martínez describes. For many of us, this experience underscores the pain and alienness of *mestizaje.* As Loida Martell-Otero says, "This is especially true of those of us who were born here. We are never recognized in our parents' country of origin (where we are 'gringos'), and we are never recognized here ('Spic, go home!')."

For such people, who are either second-class citizens or noncitizens, and who lack and miss the extended family ties that have traditionally given us a sense of belonging, the church, the "family of God," is very important. Many of us were taught an individualistic theology in which the church is an incidental result of the gospel. We hear that theology all around us, from liberal as well as from conservative sources: The church is the "service station" where we go to "gas up" for the rest of the week. The church is a voluntary gathering in which we come together in order to pool our resources to proclaim the gospel. The church is an instrument for strengthening our faith. The church is the instrument that God uses to continue proclaiming the gospel. All of this may be true; but in all of these statements, it seems that one can speak of the gospel quite apart from the church. Such are the ecclesiologies we have been taught by liberal and conservative alike. But for people whose experience of the gospel is that we "are no longer strangers and aliens, but citizens with the saints and also members of the household of God," the church is part of the gospel itself. The gospel, the good news, is not only that our sins are forgiven and we have been reconciled with God; it is also that we are now *citizens* and *family* with the saints and with God! It is in the church that we experience that. Part of the good news is that there is this new community in which, as in a foretaste of the kingdom, one can have community and extended family even in the misery of our barrios. Perhaps one could show the significance of this passage, and of the connection of alienness and family, by paraphrasing it thus: "You are no longer aliens with no papers having to hide from the *migra* [the Border Patrol and the Immigration and Naturalization Service], and strangers without roots in an extended family community; but you are citizens with the saints [which is much better than being citizens with some folk we see around us!] and members of the family of God!"

No wonder that for such people the church becomes a new extended family, in a way that the dominant culture finds difficult to understand! This is why, while in the dominant culture one often hears people speaking of "the families" in the church, in Hispanic churches the most common reference is to "the family," which is the church. Significantly, one of the values most cherished by nuclear families in the dominant culture is *privacy*—a word that does not even exist in Spanish. When they come to church, most white middle-class families wish to preserve their privacy. When they come to church, most Hispanic nuclear families come to be part of the one extended family of the church. Also significantly, when one visits a church of the dominant culture the first question one is asked is usually, "What do you do for a living?" or some version of that question. In a Hispanic church, the first question is: "Do you belong to a congregation? If so, which one?" For someone who does not understand the social ritual involved, this may seem strange. It may even be heard as the initial gambits in a proselytizing move. But what is actually taking place is a family ritual, an establishment of kinship, much as in a family reunion one might ask of a cousin, "Now, are you Aunt Millie's daughter, or Uncle Joe's?"

Hermeneutically, this means that the Bible and the history of the church are often read as a family tree. Hispanic Instructor Frances Mitchell was asked to preach at the Rio Grande Annual Conference, a United Methodist Hispanic conference in Texas and New Mexico. She used as her text the commandment in Exodus 20:12, to honor father and mother. Most sermons on this text center on the nuclear family, and are preached to young people in an effort to make them more obedient. Yet Mitchell made it clear that the commandment means much more than that. It is not just a call to respect our literal physical parents; it is also a call to honor our heritage. This heritage, as Mitchell expounded it, includes matters both cultural and ecclesiastical. To honor father and mother in the cultural context means to be true to their heritage while responding to the challenges of today. To honor mother and father in the ecclesiastical context is to remember the tradition of sacrifice from which we come—in the case of this particular sermon, the tradition of heroic sacrifice of the forerunners of the Conference—and to live as true and faithful heirs of that lineage. Again, note that in this hermeneutical approach the lines between church, family, and community tend to blur. The church is the family in which we are to honor parents. This family, though not quite coextensive with the community, potentially can include the entire community—for such is precisely the nature of the extended family.

This gives the term "family Bible" an entirely different meaning. For most people in the dominant culture, a "family Bible" is the particular copy of the Bible in which they write births, baptisms, marriages, deaths, and other such events. For us, the Bible is a "family Bible" in that it is the story of our family—not just in the few added pages were one may record a birth or a death, but from cover to cover. This is the book that tells the story of our family, the people of God. We read it, at least in part, to find out who we are. We read it, not only in private, but also out loud, in community, because this is also the book that builds our family. Many of us carry it, not only because we are about to read it in church, but also as a sign of recognition— much as among our native ancestors many clans wore distinctive colors as a means of recognition. Thus, when we see others with the same family book, we know that they are family.

The experience of exile and alienness, joined with the emphasis on (extended) family and community, has another significant hermeneutical corollary: precisely because we have the experience of exclusion we see the inclusiveness of Jesus' life and teaching, and we are called to do likewise. Commenting on the Samaritan woman at the well, David Maldonado says—as many have said before—that "Jesus often did the unexpected. He crossed lines and overcame barriers that humans had built." But then he moves beyond that, to interpret the woman's subsequent actions in a way that clearly reflects the Latino experience of exiles who have been granted a home, or of people previously excluded who have fund a wide and inclusive family:

> Jesus reached out to her across all the social and ethnic barriers. His act of reaching out to her and his words of God's gift freed her from the confining roles of her world. Because of her experience at the well, she dared to speak to all the townspeople—men and women.[3]

Furthermore, Maldonado points out, this movement from exile to homecoming goes full circle, for "the Jew [Jesus] who had once been denied hospitality in Samaria was asked to stay—and he did, for two days."[4] Significantly, as the group of Instructors discussed this passage and Maldonado's interpretation, the parallelism was drawn between the Samaritan woman and Moses. Just as Moses, after the encounter with the burning bush, goes back to his people for their liberation, so does the woman, after the encounter with Jesus, go back to her people for their liberation. An important common denominator here is the importance of one's people for one's own religious obedience and fulfillment.

The actions of Moses after the experience of the burning bush, and of the Samaritan woman after her encounter with Jesus, are both acts of solidarity. They find God, not in order "to enjoy him forever," but in order to go back to their people to do the work of God with and among them.

In the sermon on the monument at Gilgal quoted in the last chapter, the preacher went on to highlight the solidarity involved in that passage:

> As we read the entire story of the crossing of the Jordan, we may be surprised to find that all twelve tribes crossed the river. The tribes of Reuben and of Gad, and half the tribe of Mannasseh, already had lands on the other side of the Jordan. They had reached their land of promise. They had no need to cross the river. But in spite of that they too, leaving the safety and comfort of their lands, leaving their plantings and crops, cross the river with the other tribes. . . . They do not cross out of need, but out of solidarity. They cross in order to join the efforts of those other tribes that still have no land. That is why in the monument of Gilgal there are twelve stones.
>
> The same is true of our monument and our history. We are not all at the same stage in our pilgrimage. Some have prestige, power, money. According to the canons of the world, they have almost arrived. Some have a profound spiritual life. According to the canons of a certain kind of religiosity, they have almost arrived. But the truth is that there are still among our people others, many, the majority, still living in poverty and misery. And there are others, many, the majority, living without hope and without God in the world.
>
> In this world and this society, that is generally expected. We live in a world and a society in which each takes care of "number one." The rest, as the saying goes, "Que se los lleve el Diablo"—the Devil might as well take.
>
> But, Jesus tells us, not so among us. Among us, any who wish to be first must be a servant of all others. Among us, the greatest is not the one with most power, but the one who serves most. And thus, by having the tribes that have lands cross the river with those who lack them, by means of solidarity between those who have and those who

have not, between those who can and those who cannot, a new people shall be born, a new holy nation unto the Lord our God.

Our monument shall have many different stones in order to signify, not only our diversity, but also our solidarity. Our monument shall have different stones, because the smallest stone, even the minutest grain of sand, is infinitely valuable before God's eyes. If we exclude anyone, we exclude ourselves. If we forget anyone, we forget ourselves. We are one body, so that when one member rejoices we all rejoice as one, and when one member suffers we all suffer as one.[5]

What all of this means is that the unity of Christians is not for us, as for so many in the dominant culture, a matter of strategy, a means to achieve our ends. We do not come together only because "there is strength in numbers." Nor do we come together out of a sense of duty, as in the phrase, "the unity God wills," so often heard in ecumenical circles dominated by a North Atlantic worldview. We come together because for us that is part of the gospel. It is part of the gospel, not because we have been taught that in Sunday school or in membership classes, but rather because that is how we have experienced the good news of Jesus Christ. We who were exiled aliens, homeless foreigners, have found a family and a community and a people. That is good news!

We Call This Book Good

The Bible has been so good to us!" brother Avitia said. The following week I attended a worship service in which the preacher referred to what "the Good Book says." The first statement was made in the context of a group of Latinos discussing what the Bible meant to them; the second, in a mostly White, English-speaking suburban congregation. Thus, it would seem that both groups are entirely in agreement: the Bible is good.

But, does the word *good* have the same meaning in the two contexts. What the preacher meant was that the Bible is good because it teaches us what is good, and provides sound moral guidance. What Avitia meant—without discarding the moral guidance that there is in the Bible—was that the Bible is "good" because "it has been good to us." Most of the preceding chapters have described an experience that is essentially negative—marginality, poverty, mestizaje, exile, and alienness. Yet in each of those contexts we have seen that, even in the midst of pain, the Bible is good to us. Thus we read the Bible, not primarily to find out what we are to do, but to find out who we are and who we are to be. The Bible is good to us in that it answers those questions with a word of hope and affirmation.

When the preacher I have just mentioned called the Bible "the

Good Book," he was showing himself to be the heir of a long tradition that reads the Scriptures primarily as a book of instruction for the good life. Within that tradition, the most important contribution of the Bible is guidance for our lives. Thus, if we must make an important decision, we go to the Bible for an indication of the path we are to take. Our daily devotions, usually in the morning, are designed to study the Bible in order to learn how we are to behave when faced by the various circumstances of daily living. There are even people who use the Bible as a sort of magical oracle, opening it at random and then doing whatever they believe the particular passage on which their eyes land is telling them to do.

Others read the Bible as a source of information. What is the difference between an angel and an archangel? With the proper "tools," we may find the answer to that and thousands of other questions like it. Most often, these questions have to do with the end times, and the order of the last events. Are we living under the fifth, or the sixth trumpet? Is the restoration of Israel a sign that the end is about to come? Or, in a more sophisticated level, what does the Bible tell us about the nature of God or the nature of the world?

Both of these readings are valuable—at least in most cases, when we avoid the extremes of reading the Bible as an oracle or as a dictionary of last things. It is good and proper to look to the Bible for guidance in our daily lives. It is also good and proper to ask ourselves what the Bible says about God, about creation, and about the purpose of human existence. Also, both of these readings—in their legitimate as well as in their more extreme forms—are quite common in the Hispanic community.

Yet both of these common readings are insufficient in the situation of most Hispanics—and therefore I would not consider them readings "through Hispanic eyes," in the sense that we have been using those terms here.

To read the Bible as a book of guidance, as many do, implies that one is free to make all sorts of choices about one's life. Naturally, none of us is entirely devoid of choices, and therefore there is a place for such reading. But for those whose choices are often limited by social, economic, and other factors well beyond their reach, such a reading is insufficient. If I am a young man whose only choice, at least for the foreseeable future, is to work in agriculture as a migrant, it is highly unlikely that I will read the Bible asking what career I should pursue, as many of my contemporaries will be doing in a Sunday evening youth meeting in a suburban church. If I am Delia—the young woman we met in another chapter, who was unable to pay the rent for her apartment—it is highly unlikely that I will ask the Bible for guidance as to whether to go to work or not, as many women my age in a women's circle will be doing in that same suburban church.

To read the Bible seeking information may be a very enlightening exercise, but it also implies that I have the leisure to seek such enlightenment. Obviously, there is some information that all find valuable, and therefore all Christians read the Bible, at least to some degree, in that fashion. But curiosity is a luxury that only the idle can afford. Those who must constantly work for a minimum living have little time to be curious—much less to be interested—about fine points of doctrine or theology. Thus, if I am a refugee who has come to these lands looking for freedom from oppression and from poverty, and who must spend all my time either working or looking for work, it is highly improbable that I shall have the time for idle curiosity about some point of doctrine, or about whether the restoration of Israel has eschatological significance—except insofar as I use such curiosity as a way to escape from my present and constant predicament, much as an addict uses alcohol or many in our society use sports.

But there is a third sort of reading that is more typical of what we have seen in the preceding pages. This is a reading in which we go to the Scriptures, not primarily for guidance or for information, but rather for insight and strength. When the poor read the Bible, they do not find there a blueprint for escaping their poverty—even though many preachers continually tell them that it is so. What they find is rather a worldview, and an interpretation of their own predicament, that put things under a new light and give them a new sense of worth and of hope. It is no longer true, as I was told, that the reason why I am poor is that I do not work as hard as others in our society. It is no longer true, as I was told, that my poverty is willed by God, so that to rebel or strive against it is an ungodly act. It is no longer true that God destined some to be poor and some to be rich. It is no longer true that the rich or the nonpoor are closer to God, simply because they dress better and live in bigger houses.

This is what we mean when we say that the Bible is good to us. It is not so much that we interpret the Bible, as that the Bible interprets us in a radically new and ultimately affirming way! The Bible tells us, no matter how crushed we might be, that we are a royal priesthood! The Bible tells us, no matter how rootless and homeless society might make us feel, that we are part of God's own family, and of the great home that God is building. The Bible tells us, no matter whether we have green cards or not, that we are citizens of the New Jerusalem. Thus, when you see us walking to church early on a Sunday morning, and wonder at the loving tenderness with which we cradle our Bibles in our arms, know that we do this, not out of some fanatical bibliolatry, but simply out of love and gratitude, because indeed *the Bible has been good to us!*

NOTES

Preface

1. These materials are on file at the offices of the Mexican American Program, Perkins School of Theology, Southern Methodist University.

Introduction

1. Some of this material was delivered as a lecture at the University of Chicago Divinity School, October 27, 1994, as part of the Centennial Hoover Lectures of the Disciples Divinity House.

2. I have explored this subject in an article, "Metamodern Aliens in Postmodern Jerusalem," in *Aliens in Jerusalem*. Ada María Isasi-Díaz and Fernando Segovia, eds. (Philadelphia: Fortress, 1996), and in a series of lectures delivered recently at Western Theological Seminary, which I am currently preparing for publication.

3. Throughout this book, I use the terms "Hispanic" and "Latino" as fully interchangeable. Although there is much debate among Hispanics/Latinos about which name is better, the fact is that neither is fully satisfactory. See "What's in a Name," in J. L. González, ed., *Each in Our Own Tongue: A History of Hispanic United Methodism* (Nashville: Abingdon, 1991), pp. 22-23; Ada María Isasi-Díaz, "Naming Ourselves," in *En la Lucha: In the Struggle: Elaborating a Mujerista Theology* (Minneapolis: Fortress, 1993), pp. 2-4. Here we see the wisdom in the words of Orlando O. Espín in the very first issue of the *Journal of Hispanic/Latino Theology* (Nov. 1993, p. 4):

the continuing discussion among our communities on the more adequate "name" for ourselves has led the journal to choose its somewhat awkward title

119

(*Hispanic/Latino*). We want this periodical's name to signify inclusion and respect.

4. A point that I have elaborated more fully in *Out of Every Tribe and Nation: Christian Theology at the Ethnic Roundtable* (Nashville: Abingdon, 1992), pp. 18-27.

5. Sandra M. Schneiders, *The Revelatory Text: Interpreting the New Testament as Sacred Scripture* (San Francisco: HarperCollins, 1991), p. 21.

6. For my non-Methodist readers, allow me to explain that it was in a chapel on Aldersgate Street that Wesley, upon hearing a reading from Luther's preface to Romans, felt his heart "strangely warmed," and came to the conviction that his sins had been truly forgiven. Although Wesley did not speak often of the Aldersgate experience, Methodists have come to see it as the turning point in his life.

7. Catherine Gunsalus González and Justo Luis González, *Their Souls Did Magnify the Lord: Studies on Biblical Women* (Atlanta: General Assembly Mission Board, 1977).

Chapter 1

1. These words appear in the context of the conversion of Levi, which may be read as another instance of how religious folk are willing to accept repentant sinners, so long as there are not too many of them. One can well imagine that the Pharisees would have no objection to the conversion of Levi. After all, here was a publican changing his way of life. But now it appears that the door through which Levi has entered is becoming too wide. Jesus has opened his fellowship, not only to Levi, but also to a multitude of other publicans and sinners. And this makes the Pharisees cringe.

Chapter 2

1. From a sermon by Daniel García as part of the Hispanic Instructors Program, Perkins School of Theology, Southern Methodist University.

2. A. N. Sherwin-White, *Roman Society and Roman Law in the New Testament* (Oxford: Oxford University Press, 1963), pp. 134-36.

3. G. H. C. Macgregor, *The New Interpreter's Bible* (Abingdon: Nashville, 1982), vol. 9, p. 73.

4. J. A. Ziesler, *Christian Asceticism* (Grand Rapids: Eerdmans, 1973), p. 110.

5. From a sermon by Yolanda Pupo-Ortiz as part of the Hispanic

Instructors Program, Perkins School of Theology, Southern Methodist University.

Chapter 3

1. It is interesting to note that the manner in which this distinction was kept between the "mestizo" and the "mulatto" was by drawing these terms from words with the same meaning, one the Latin *mixticius* and the other the Arab *muwallad.*

2. In the sixteenth century many considered being of mixed parentage—as long as it was noble on both sides—a matter of pride. Notable among the writers of the time was "El Inca" Garcilaso de la Vega, related to the ancient royal house of Peru through his mother, as well as to the minor Spanish nobility through his father—and he boasted of both parentages.

3. His dissertation title was *Mestissage, violence culturelle, annonce de l'évangile.* There is an English translation: *Mestizaje: The Dialectics of Cultural Birth and the Gospels* (San Antonio: Mexican American Cultural Center, 1978). His best known book, *Galilean Journey,* was published by Orbis in 1983. He later expanded the implications of his theory of mestizaje in *The Future is Mestizo: Life Where Cultures Meet* (Bloomington, Ind.: Meyer Stone Books, 1988).

4. *Galilean* Journey (Maryknoll, N.Y.: Orbis Books, 1983), p. 18.

5. Ibid., pp. 98-99.

6. "Double Dutch: Reflections of an Hispanic-North American on Multicultural Religious Education," *Apuntes,* vol. VIII, No. 2 (Summer 1988), p. 27.

7. Portions of this section on Saul/Paul and his mestizaje have been adapted from a sermon on Acts 13:9 that I preached at the 159th Commencement of McCormick Theological Seminary, and published as "View from the Crossroads," in *McCormick Perspectives,* Fall 1993, pp. 1-3.

8. Actually, a Roman citizen would have three names: the *praenomen,* the *nomen,* and the *cognomen.* "Paul" was probably his *cognomen.* His *praenomen,* which would have been his personal name by which he would be addressed by his family, is unknown. So is his *nomen,* which would indicate his family relationship—much as our modern "last name." Besides these three, many people, especially in the eastern part of the empire, had a fourth name, the *supernomen* or *signum.* This was used by their intimates, especially in connection

with a non-Graecoroman culture and language. "Saul" was probably such a *supernomen*.

9. Part of what follows is adapted from my article "Where Frontiers End . . . and Borders Begin," in *Basta!* (National Journal of the Chicago Religious Task Force on Central America), February 1990, pp. 19-22.

Quoted from García-Treto, "The Lesson of the Gibeonites: A Proposal for Dialogic Attention as a Strategy for Reading the Bible," to be published in the currently titled *Aliens in Jerusalem*, Ada María Isasi-Díaz and Fernando Segovia, eds. (Philadelphia: Fortress, 1996), p. 1.

11. Ibid.

12. "Joshua," in Carol A. Newsom and Sharon H. Ringe, eds., *The Woman's Bible Commentary* (Louisville: Westminster/John Knox Press, 1992), p. 63.

13. *Undergods and Tricksters: A Prelude to Biblical Folklore* (San Francisco: Harper & Row, 1987).

14. García-Treto, p. 13.

15. Ibid., p. 15.

16. From an unpublished sermon by Loida Martell-Otero.

Chapter 4

1. Francisco O. García-Treto, "El Señor guarda a los emigrantes," *Apuntes,* vol. I, no. 4 Winter 1981, p. 4.

2. Ibid., pp. 6-7.

3. Jorge Lara-Braud, "Reflexiones teológicas sobre la migración," *Apuntes,* vol. II, no. 1, Spring 1982, pp. 3-7.

4. Ibid., p. 5.

5. See Robert M. Grant, *Gnosticism and Early Christianity* (New York: Schoken Books, 1961), pp. 39-69.

6. Eldin Villafañe, *Seek the Welfare of the City: Reflections on Urban Ministry* (in preparation for press).

7. In the introductory chapter to S*eek the Welfare*. Also in Villafañe, "The Jeremiah Paradigm for the City," *Christianity and Crisis,* Nov. 16, 1992, p. 374.

8. Jorge González, in a yet unpublished commentary on Jeremiah.

9. Justo González, *Punto de Apoyo,* a publication of the Hispanic Ministries Program of McCormick Theological Seminary, vol. II, no. 6-7, Nov.-Dec. 1994, p.3.

10. Ibid., pp. 1, 3.

Chapter 5

1. John H. Elliott, *A Home for the Homeless: A Social-Scientific Criticism of First Peter, Its Situation and Strategy* (Minneapolis: Fortress, 1990).
2. "In Search of an Inclusive Community," *Apuntes,* vol. IX, no. 1, p. 4.
3. *The Upper Room Disciplines,* March 13, 1993.
4. Ibid.
5. In *Punto de Apoyo,* vol. II, no. 6-7, Nov.-Dec. 1994, p. 4.